WHAT'S NEXT
AFTER NOW?

WHAT'S NEXT AFTER NOW?

POST-SPIRITUALITY AND THE CREATIVE LIFE

STEVEN HARRISON

SENTIENT PUBLICATIONS, LLC

First Sentient Publications edition 2005
Copyright © 2005 by Steven Harrison

A paperback original

Printed in the United States of America

Cover design by Kim Johansen, Black Dog Design
Book design by Nicholas Cummings

Library of Congress Cataloging-in-Publication Data is available at the Library of Congress

10 9 8 7 6 5 4 3 2 1

SENTIENT PUBLICATIONS, LLC
1113 Spruce Street
Boulder, CO 80302
www.sentientpublications.com

CONTENTS

INTRODUCTION

The seeker set off into the forest to find a yogi of great renown. Eventually he came upon the hermit sitting in silence and sat before him. After some time, hoping to test the master, the seeker said, "Is this a question?" And the yogi replied, "If that is a question, then this is an answer."

OUR SEARCH FOR UNDERSTANDING HAS BEEN DEFINED FOR MILlennia as an ever-expanding construction of more and more complex concepts. Since the beginning of recorded history, we have asked questions suggested by our natural world and the increasingly intricate social structure we have created as human beings. We have mythologized the expansion of understanding as a never-ending quest for the ultimate answers, as if we had the capacity to ask the ultimate questions.

What this myth could not take into account is the possibility that our understanding would come to the end of its own capacity and that understanding itself, not just its content, must undergo a transformation. Expansion is not the only direction of understanding; it just happens to be the quality of our current form of it. An entirely different form of understanding may occur in the shift from one condition of the human potential to another, like an expanse of space collapsing into a black hole and emerging in a new universe. If this is the case, then the understanding we had has no bearing on the completely new kind of knowledge that emerges, and what we know now cannot be of any help in what is next.

The understanding that we have come to accept as knowledge, whether of the so-called material world or the conceptual world, cannot know more than its capacity. Individually and collectively, we are limited in our understanding by the nature of understanding itself. We can train our brains and those of our children to retain increasing amounts of information from gestation to death, we can expand beyond the limitations of our brains by using computers that run at the incredible speeds possible at the molecular level, but in the end we come to the limitation of the known.

Can we face the end of the age of reason, the limits of science, the grand finale of collecting and collating the permutations of category and utility? Can we stand in the dissolution of our mythic religions, our fable of spirituality, and the disconnected questions of our philosophies? Can we understand the boundaries of our understanding?

To do so is to face a universe unmasked, to face the very forces that we avoided by constructing our elaborate virtual world of understanding. We have dived so deeply into the mechanics of the world that we have hit the bottom of the clockwork universe worldview. With that emerges a paradigm of a universe without causality. Newtonian physics makes way for quantum physics, but what comes from the quantum reality? Acausality breeds an unrecognizable world where once there were qualities such as meaning, purpose, and distinct qualities. With cause and effect we have the immense pleasure of an understanding out of which we can build a life worth living, smug in our roots of knowledge.

We have eaten the apple, and while it has cost us para-
dise, we have the anesthesia of knowledge, so we feel nothing
of the loss. When the narcotic wears off, we are overwhelmed
by the puniness of our knowing in the face of what it is not.
What it is not is totality—an integral knowledge that is unavail-
able to our understanding and unapproachable through our
known realities of time, location, causation, and meaning.

Our understanding takes us to the end of each of these
aspects and, with that, to the end of itself, transformed in the
loss of these familiar realities. This flameout of the known suggests an entirely different modality, one that emerges from the
ashes of our understanding but cannot be characterized as
anything we understand.

What is it that emerges, what is that we are living, in the
actual, not the imagined? Are we prepared to place the constructions of our life on the fires of transformation—the
alchemical forge that destroys, purifies, melds, transforms, and
creates what is next?

In what follows is the impossibility of exploring these questions in words. With the expression of that impossibility is the
invitation for you to engage the equally impossible task of
entering into these words in a new way—not looking for content, information, or knowledge, which you will most assured-
ly not get here. It will be futile to look for logical consistency
or empirical reasoning in an inquiry into acausality. Rather,
take in what is expressed as a movement of co-creativity—a
catalyst for transformation that comes not from words, or even
from a dialog between author and reader, but from the complete abandonment of all that has been for what is next.

PART I
BREAKDOWN

THE FIRES OF TRANSFORMATION

If it is held that there is something to be realized or attained apart from mind, and thereupon, mind is used to seek it, that is failure to understand that mind and the object of its search are one. Mind cannot be used to seek something from mind for, even after the passage of millions of kalpas, the day of success would never come.

—Huang-po

SELF-DECEPTION
AND THE
FIRES
OF
TRANSFORMATION

Descartes goes into a bar and orders a beer. After he finishes his drink, the bartender asks him if he wants another one. "I think not," Descartes says. Then he disappears.

THE FUNDAMENTAL DECEPTION WE CONSTRUCT IS THE IDEA OF THE self. This prime organizing assumption is the progenitor of all the other deceptions, and it is generated by thought itself as an integral part of the arising of the thought form. By the very architecture of thinking we generate a subject-object reality in which we give automatic existence to an entity called *me,* a complex virtual character worthy of a classic science fiction novel. Utilizing the tool of thought that both generates the *me* and seeks to create the circumstance of its survival, we set about a life of thinking and surviving.

We apprehend thought as the reflection of life and believe that what we think is in some way accurate. But thought is the projector, not the reflector. It is the creator of our reality, not the mirror of it. Thought is reality, a subjective construction; the actual is something else entirely. While we are the center of this projected universe, the lack of full dimensionality in the flat world of thought suggests to us that there is something fundamentally untrue about everything. This subtle disturbance is the actuality of the universe impinging on our dream world. The awakening from the dream appears from the perspective of the dream as death.

The notion of the self is the denial of the death of our delusion—the self posits itself *to itself* over and over again, despite the continuous crumbling of reality in each moment. Somehow the self will survive through its contrivances and strategies; it will exist, however it has to.

It's fascinating that this self that doesn't exist appears to function to deny its own death and projects a universe in which it's the center and the interpreter.

No wonder we're confused.

To further the deception, thinking creates time, which has history, future, and continuity—a continuity implied in the structure of the past moving through the present into the future. The self thinks of itself as in time; time, like the notion of a center, is inextricably imbedded in the nature of thought. With time, the logic of thinking and the utility of anticipating, predicting, and measuring become an essential part of the survivability of the mythic self. Without time, the self evaporates.

Our self-deception sees all of this—clever people that we are—and smugly decides to do something about it. Self-deception begins its spiritual search to fix all of this and to connect to the truth. But our "doing" is actually in search of more self-deception, because it is in search of experience. The seeking is in search of enlightenment or love. We are searching for something that we can have that will resolve the fundamental conflict of our fear of death, our nonexistence. We deceive ourselves that this search is going to capture some essential experience that is going to change us forever. But experience is just more thought, more memory imbedded in the imaginary stream of time, described not in what actually occurred, but in what the thinker thought occurred.

The self-deception is keenly aware of these shortcomings and the fragile structure of the self-centered reality. What better remedy than to create God? God can be personal or impersonal, loving or vengeful. The essential self-deception is the same no matter what form we give to our God, in the rather inflated notion that we can know God. The *me*—the self that doesn't exist, that's afraid of death, that creates the universe through its thinking—has the idea that it knows what's going on and thereby controls it. This is why we love the God of our imagination, because God can be exactly the way we posit God to be. We can animate the animator with our own characteristics, which is a very safe God.

God is not an object. God is not available to the divided world of subject-object that the thinking self creates. Only the idea of God can be found, and the idea of God is not God.

The failure of the spiritual search and the uselessness of any action moving in time in relationship to understanding, devotion, or surrender to the divine, introduces us to the absolute—of being stuck. There is no end to the conceptual self searching in the virtual spiritual reality for the mythic enlightenment. Thought chasing its tail has no exit strategy. There is no escape, and this leaves us immersed in the fires of transformation. In this conundrum, the churning mechanism of thought continues. It has no way out of itself. It can only create experience, however sublime, which creates self, however subtle, which searches for more experience, because there is never enough.

The fires of transformation are the destruction of the elements of reality and the alchemic purification that occur not out of intention, or will, or practice, but entirely without causation, without duration, without any trace of memory or experience, without a *me*.

The introductory fire of transformation is the moment. In the attention to this moment the whole show of the self is transparent. We can see the actual arising of thought as it creates the self, the fear of death, the search for experience. It is obvious that thought characterizes reality so substantially that it is one and the same, that thought is our reality. This intense flame burns up any notion of an objective world knowable to thought.

In the moment there is no apparent time, and the absence of time is another fire of transformation. Timelessness burns all of our concepts, which are bound in the progression of past, present, and future. The idea of me is bound in process. In timelessness, in this moment, my aspirations—my efforts to improve my spirituality—are burned up. There cannot be any experience to have and none to get to in the future. What are my hopes and dreams if there are no experiences to gather? What kind of spiritual process is there when there is no time? Being in the moment is still being in illusion, still a reference to a world of time in which we can be in or out of a storybook now. If there is no time, there is no now.

Seeing the creation of self in time and process, we enter another fire, which is the fire of interconnectedness. We have been attempting to drive our lives from a center that is nonexistent. The glimpse of no self introduces us to a life lived from the whole of life, not just from an aspect. Thought keeps arising—the world of subject-object continues to arise with each thought—but this is not the organizing principle; it is rather an expression of that whole. Yet this glimpse is not enough to transform our life.

There is the fire of surrender. We no longer maintain the illusion of control of our life through the idea of free will. If thought is directing life, then what is directing thought? We recognize the mechanical and conditioned nature of thought, the fact that it's secondhand, and that its relentless arising and passing away is acausal. The fire of surrender is of particular intensity; it is remorseless in its demand that we accept what is and step fully into what is next.

When we are faced with the fires of transformation, the wholeness of life, the actuality-just-as-it-is, the surety of mind crumbles, leaving us with the apparent acausality of the moment. Yet, this is the ultimate self-deception: the idea that something profound is happening. We have the idea that we are going through some kind of spiritual transformation. Self-deception can even create a conceptual reality about wholeness—a world within a world that is bigger than what we were, but still contained within thought. ·

The world of thought is the world of experience, in which this moment of stillness becomes captured by memory. It's now incorporated into *me*. I just had that moment of stillness, of reflection, and that makes me better. It improves my situation, makes me more whole. It might even make me happier. The world of experience is an approximation and nothing more. Whatever we come to, today or ever, is not "it." Whatever we find we will have to discard. Whatever we come to is gone. Even this moment must be discarded.

This means that the experiencer, the central organizing principal of our life, has no function when it comes to understanding wholeness. The *me* can't have it. It can have a telephone number, it can have an address, it can have the knowledge of how to run a computer program, it can have a lot of

11

things. But it cannot have wholeness. Thought cannot contain the whole, only the thought of the whole.

This brings us to what appears to be the final fire of transformation, which is nonexistence. There is nothing to experience and no experiencer. There is no fragment, no whole, no relative, no absolute. There is no self-deception and no fire of transformation. There is nothing and not nothing. We cannot approach this fire and we cannot escape it.

Thought continues to arise, more intensely in the face of nonexistence. But thought cannot describe accurately, nor can it direct us meaningfully, in the flow of the actuality of life. Will we live from that fragment called thought, although it is not actual? Thought appears to be something we can rely on because it is mechanical, but it is only an aspect. Do we live from the idea of wholeness—what is often called spirituality, but is still in the realm of ideas? Are we content with the collection of concepts, memories, experiences, or is the wild, unfettered, unpredictable, unbelievable, uncontrollable energy of life calling? Do we live from the dynamic whole, which is not necessarily from our preferences, doesn't necessarily bring us what we desire, and can be anything at any time?

As children we liked to ride on the mechanical horse at the shopping center. We put in a penny and the horse rocked back and forth, something like a real horse. For all we knew as children, it was probably pretty close to an actual horse. But it is not the same thing as riding a horse, let alone a wild horse. Once we know this, is it enough to put in a penny and know that the pretend horse will rock us back and forth in a predictable way and that we are not likely to fall off? We can pretend excitement; we can imagine the wind against our faces, the fear, the energy, and the wildness of the unknown ride. Is that pretend world enough? And if it is not enough, could we make do with the memory that we once rode a real horse and remember that past as we rock on the mechanical one? Or how about a movie or book on riding wild horses? At what point do we need the actual so intensely that we abandon all replications, outer and inner?

Is it satisfactory to have the occasional experience of still-ness to which we can then refer? Is it enough to read about the pathways to transformation of others? It is a pleasant kind of self-deception. The fires of transformation burn just at the edges of this illusion.

Is it self-deception or the fires of transformation? The fires are unlimited. They burn every moment in a different way. They are not predictable. They are not knowable. We don't know if there will be extreme pleasure, extreme pain, some-thing in between, or nothing.

Where do we find the answer to the fundamental question of what we want? We know the spiritually correct answer is to want transformation, but that right answer is also a concept. Where do we find the full answer to the whole question?

There is a deep feeling in us that is not concept and not emotion—something that is actually living, dynamic, moving, changing—that lives in us and through us. This is the final fire, emerging out of the abyss of nonexistence and flaming through the ever-arising thought world and all that is non-thought.

This is the fire of the heart. Love is the quality that we fear the most, because it has nothing to do with this me. It is the death that we feared when we began constructing the whole world of mind. It is ironic that it is not really death we fear; it is love, it is life, it is connection. But the love, the life, the con-nection does not need the boundaries of our constructs. This energy can use our mind, our body, our being, but it doesn't need it. It is not me-centric; it has no center. It is the final fire, because it is in fact the death of the entire construct out of which we have been living. Yet it is fully alive in that death, and the fire is no longer destructive but immensely creative. From this creativity emerges what is next.

When we start to see this we want to know how to continue in the process. But are we going to continue to work on seeing it, or are we going to give expression to what we see? We see the structures of mind create a self-centered universe, but we want that self-deception because it's comfortable and apparently safe. Certainly the self-deception has a little bit of pain built into it with the idea of death, but we can utilize our spirituality to create more time while we're working on it. If we have seen all of this, what's next? Or do we go back to see it again just to be sure? Does the seeing it now become a habit in itself?

We may say that we want our life to be an expression of love. We certainly love our concepts. We don't want to let go of them. We like what we have while we pretend that we don't. Apparently we accept what accompanies this me—the pain that is inherent in the construction of a self, the divided world that it creates, and the unreality of the projected mind and all the illusion that spins from it.

We think we can choose not to be in the conceptual world; that idea is still within the conceptual. We can give up the whole idea of choice by seeing that it has no function at all; it is disconnected from the actual, which is without causation. The whole "choosing" show is in the mind as an entertainment feature that keeps us occupied while we maintain a separate existence and the sense of survivability. That realm has nothing to do with what is actual. Mind cannot choose to find the fire of love; love does the choosing. Our life of separation was constructed out of the thinking and choosing mechanism. If we see its lack of actuality, that whole life that we've been living unravels. We certainly don't want that, which is why self-deception is very handy. Through the mechanisms of self-deception, we can get up out of our chair, go someplace, and have something to do that is meaningful. We can have our pain and our conflict that goes with it. That is a fine byproduct so long as we have meaning.

We believe that our life would not work without the endless churning of decision-making and characterizing, focused on the survivability of this particular self. The actuality of life is unfathomable to this particular mind, yet we are convinced that life cannot work without our comprehension of it. This is absurd.

The consideration that life is not operated by the thinking mechanism is a little terrifying. We can see that life utilizes the thinking mechanism, but life does not require the thinking mechanism to animate it. This is radical in this respect: we are living in the unknown, whether we are thinking about it or not. Thankfully, not knowing is the portal to possibility.

The personal aspect becomes largely dysfunctional in this light unless it can intertwine with the whole. We cannot continue to organize ourselves in a divided way, because the quality we metaphorically call love is now permeating our life.

The identification with thought-as-me will try to reassert itself over and over again, because that is what it does. The *me* of the mechanism does not want to do anything about that, other than create the spiritual process, which creates time. When we recognize the endless corrective process of the mind structure and its non-utility, we have stepped into another world. The unknown is the animating and we are the animated. We can no longer inquire into it from the perspective of the conceptual, because we've recognized that we are not that. We are left inquiring from the non-located perspective. The psychological self will attempt to return to the self-centered, psychological inquiry. If we find ourselves in the loop of spirituality, let's recognize that is what we are doing to occupy ourselves with apparent meaning.

The normal life is the result of this conditioned circumstance in which we have all found ourselves. We are not discarding the normal or reacting to it. Rather, there is a merger of the conditioning and the awareness of it into something that is new. If our life is completely available to the movement of unindividuated consciousness, it is not a normal life anymore, and at the same time it is nothing special at all. We can no longer say that we are aware, because we cannot stand outside of awareness to claim it.

There is not a choice there, not two possible worlds. In actuality, there is not awareness and a normal life; these are words. There is only one thing. And that one thing is completely alive and contains all possibilities in it. We have merged with life—completely dynamic and fluid.

Everything that we can apprehend is self-deceiving. Start with that, and we won't miss any self-deception. Everything that we know, everything that we can characterize, everything that we can judge, everything that we can express, is self-deception.

We may suppose that it is a process of catching the creation of thought through awareness and that the more we catch it, the less the conceptual framework seems attractive. Process is part of the self-deception—even the process of becoming more aware. We forge our relationship and construct our life around the immediacy of the fires of transformation, not the more and more of getting better. This is not necessarily a comfortable relationship—it is not the gauzy love of a romantic movie—but it burns with authenticity.

This is why we bounce off so many relationships. The initial part is the attraction, then we find the place that doesn't feel good, and off we go looking for what feels better. It is the same thing with our gods, our religions, and our spirituality. Once we hit that point of challenge, we follow the reaction that gets us out of there. We didn't come for transformation. We came to feel good.

Can we stand still in every relationship, in everything we touch? Can we surrender to the actual qualities that are occurring and let them do their work on us? All those qualities will pass through our system, sandblasting, and take away all the veneer. It doesn't feel good or bad if you are still. It just is. It is when you try to fix it, or to characterize it, or to understand it, or to conceptualize it that it starts to feel good or bad. If it's good, you'll want more of it, and over-consume. If it's bad, you'll run from it, missing the contact.

We construct conceptual frameworks to locate ourselves so we don't experience the fear of what is implied in having no location. Do we have any interest in finding out what happens if we don't construct this center? Or are we just looking for a more sophisticated layer because the old one wore off? We have to get stronger and stronger conceptual drugs to keep us located.

When you observe children, provided that they are not inundated by concepts, you see that they participate in life very naturally and fully. In a way, children are fluid because they don't really have a set idea yet of who they are or of what they are supposed to be. They just have the movement of energy through them. You can see them try on all kinds of personalities in a day, in an hour, in a moment. They can go everywhere, from the most sublime sweetness to the most ter-rible rage. For them, nothing says this is good or bad until we, the adults in their world, say this is good and this is bad. Then they begin forming their relationship to that.

But, we aren't children, nor can we to return to a child-like state. Then what? We think that maybe it's a matter of elimi-nating ideas, rather than the acquisition of them. Let's get rid of all the ideas. They're gone. Now what?

We reach a place where there is just nothing. It seems that in a moment it accidentally happened. Then the next moment there is something.

Let's find out about nothing, then. We don't need con-cepts. Nothing is required. No action is required. Shall we fig-ure out how to make that accident happen all the time?

We could say that accidental moment was pleasurable, it was expansive, it was open. What follows that open moment is closed or restricted, less pleasurable.

There is something going on in the background all the time that qualifies the pleasurable as *we want it* and the unpleasant as *we don't*. Judgment threads through those two kinds of experiences, constructing your life. It is trying to find more of that accidental pleasure and less of that mechanical pain. It apprehends the likes and dislikes and constructs around them. You don't need to know it's there; it's just operating in the background. Judgment is pushing us forward, pulling us back.

But now it's been revealed, and here's the conundrum: what does judgment do with itself? Does it pull back from itself, or push into itself? Is the organizing principle pleasurable or painful? Can it answer the question of whether it is, itself, pleasurable or painful?

Take this into your sense of the moment, not as a philo-sophical stance, not as a conceptual idea. What is the direct experience, now? Can you feel the pressure of the floor on your feet? The sounds around you? The tensions in the body? Is the experience qualified or bare? Do you characterize what occurs, or is it simply the actuality without commentary?

We have the sensate experience of the body and the analysis of that. We have the attempt to stop analyzing that and some dissatisfaction or irritation. There is something aware of that whole bundle of activity.

What if we don't follow that process? Can we see directly what our experience is without trying to modify it, improve it, change it, condition it—without searching for the pleasure, pushing away the pain?

We constantly generate descriptions by which we live. We know that life is not contained within the conceptual realm, it's not described accurately by those ideas, yet we still live in relationship to those descriptions.

We have the challenge to express the unknown—an impossible challenge. All we know about it is what it's not; we don't know a thing about what it is. There is no way of knowing now, or at any point in the future, what the expression of the unknown is. This is why from the conceptual perspective, which is designed to know, it's frightening and futile.

This is the moment of transformation. At every moment we have the capacity to fall back into the defended space of the known and we have the ability to abandon the moment and enter into the unknown of what is next.

Let us face the full range of the human potential by engaging the fear of a negative expression and the attraction of a positive expression, both of which are terrifying. We are as afraid of our love as we are of our anger.

The expression is a deep feeling—not feeling in terms of emotion, which is also conditioned, just like thought is—but feeling that is the totality of the energetic movement in the system, expressing itself through some aspect.

That is a radical life. While it is fresh and alive, it may be totally unrecognizable to us to be completely authentic in every moment.

We don't want to break down into an unfettered expression. We always want to recognize *me* in the world. We always want to know where we are. We don't have any interest in the unconditioned. Our interest is to have a location at all times, know where we are, be in control, and make sure we don't take any risks with each other.

Is that enough in life? That's a dangerous question, and we avoid that question as much as possible. We have developed extensive philosophies around that, including the notion of a selfless universe that animates us. Because as the stakes get higher and higher we must develop greater and greater defenses.

We are just not interested in that place where the *me* cannot go. We will go to any level of realization, any way we need to, including the weirdest religions and spirituality, as long as we are still there in the end. But if we are not going to be there, we are not going, and no one can convince us or take us there.

We have created these logical, emotional, and interpersonal systems that are impenetrable. There is no way out of that. Spirituality won't help. We work toward having the Zen experience, the rebirth experience, the enlightenment experience. Working toward that spiritual ideal of a world without *me* could fill up our whole life. Before that, we were stuck with just me—all that repetitive noise, feeling dense and painful, without meaning or purpose. Now that we have become spiritual, we know the *me* is a terrible illusion, but we certainly don't want a world without me. A world that doesn't have me in it is a very dangerous world. It's the most dangerous of all worlds, from my perspective. From your perspective, the most dangerous world is a world without you. But from my perspective a world without you is fine.

THE ONE
TRUE
ACTION

SELF-DECEPTION IS THE CREATION OF AN IDENTITY, A LOCATION, YOU and me, and the attempt to escape through the spirituality of self-improvement. Ultimately, we seek enlightenment—freedom from the whole game that we've created. Yet there is a gnawing knowing that the whole thing is a setup; it's a creation that has no out and no reality to it.

This was clearly laid out to me by my young children one day. The one teases the other, who then responds by saying *stop it,* only creating more teasing. And more *stop it.* And more teasing and more *stop it* and more teasing.

It is much like the arising of thought, creating the sense of self, creating the irritation of separation, creating the inclination to stop that irritation and to love, to be whole. And then the fear of wholeness arising, saying, *If it's whole, what about me?* It is an endless cycle.

My advice, of course, to my children is a version of doing nothing. Ignore the teasing. Ignore the whole show. Of course, these children are expert provocateurs, much as our thoughts are impossible to ignore.

I tried just being with the children in their conflict. I am supposed to be able to do this, but I found it actually intensely irritating. I am supposed to be collecting some kind of sensibility so that I can transmit something that is peaceful or profound, instead of being overloaded by kids bickering.

My kids don't care about profundity, unfortunately. And so, they overwhelm each other and me. I would like to be peaceful, but I find that the tension between the peacefulness and the bickering becomes a kind of macro-tension.

When doing nothing does not work, then I might suggest to them a kind of tantric approach, which is to ride the energy of competition and conflict. Let's see which child can be the quietest until we get where we are going. This sets up a competition between children—much like our spirituality sets up a competition—to be the stillest, the quietest, the one who can sit the longest, the one who has the deepest experience. This actually works with children for a while, just as it does for seekers for a while. It gets very quiet and serene, and one feels the self-congratulation of superior parenting. Then, of course, we arrive, and there is a burst of the opposite, an intensification of teasing and reaction.

This is much like when we return to daily life from our meditation retreats, where we found such depth, or our yoga weekends, where we stretched into near samadhi. When we go on a retreat, we get very sublime. Then when we step back into our life, the problems seem to be even worse, and the best of our life doesn't seem to be quite as good since we've experienced such expansion on retreat. This is another kind of endless cycle.

We find ourselves in this dilemma as human beings. What do we do about all of it? What is the fire of transformation that burns the whole thing up? What is it that doesn't just suppress it, doesn't modify it, but destroys it?

I'd like to be observing my life, but it doesn't stop the conflict. So all my observation is creating separation and the problem of the detached watcher. The fact is that I am not observing my life; I'm actually in it. I can't separate.

The actuality of our life is that we are attached. We're passionate. We're connected to our family, our kids, our friends, and our workplace. This is not like a spiritual meeting, where we can easily stay detached and cool with each other. In the hotness, in the energy of our actual life, we can't observe, we can only be drawn in. There is no hope of a spiritual sensibility; we collapse into the muck of our actual life. In this spiritual hopelessness there is great freedom. We can see clearly that there is nothing we can do and that absolute non-doing is the relationship to it all, yet there is sometimes an urgency to take an action. Sometimes there is the sense of no action. Is it just a mechanical happenstance, just a random unfolding of events, or does the flow of doing and non-doing have intelligence? There is no escape from the dynamic of life.

We've learned along the way of the spiritual path that we're supposed to be observing. Somewhere prior to this learning, we might have been observing and not knowing that we were supposed to or even that it was called observing. We just happened to be doing it. But now we are doing it because we were told to do it, we learned to do it, and we think it's good.

As an experiment, don't step back from life through observation. We thought we could get away from life by observing, but life is tremendously energetic. Now we are in the fray, in the movement of whatever is occurring.

We construct our life around peacefulness as a state and thereby say we're getting better. We are really removing anything that can challenge the peacefulness. Can you take your peacefulness into an attached world? Or is your understanding,

your peacefulness, your state of mind only good in certain circumstances?

You may think that if your peacefulness is real, it is good
anywhere. If so, are you available for childcare?

Does your abiding peacefulness in relationship to the phenomenology of life stand up in the face of qualities that are
truly overwhelming? How does it hold up when confronted
with a child in a tantrum, a loved one dying, profound illness,
financial calamity, or the collapse of everything that you have
constructed as security in your life? At the far end of that spec-
trum of disruption is your death. This is the cessation of the
entire construction—everything that you're attached to and
everything that you're adverse to. Seeing the very structure of
yourself as thought, you can also see your death, because you
can see the arising and the passing away of the entire structure. That's not necessarily at the end of the physical life, but
it is a death that plunges you into nonexistence.

The real challenge in relationship to my children is my
death and their death, the death of the whole theatre piece,
the show that I'm the father and they are my children, that I
have important work to do, that I am a wise parent, that what
I have to say to them has meaning and purpose. In death, the
whole construction is consumed by fire.

If I take what I know and we throw it into the fire of the
unknown, what is left? What can my knowledge actually face?
My understanding does very well as long as it's confronting the
world that I construct. But can it face the world that I don't
construct? What in my construction can truly face the end of
me? At some point when the physical body breaks down and
therefore doesn't support the conceptual world, this thing
called me simply ceases, along with the passions, the regrets,
and all the rest of it.

Is there some urgency that is moving through us? Because the fact of our life is not that we are just passive and satisfied. We're not just in that flow; we have the companion of irritation. At some point, the question comes up—can I step out of the whole drama right now? Is it an action? Is it passive? Is there any energy that is pushing me?

We all have management techniques in our repertoire for the conflicts in our life. Is there some way to step completely out of the whole thing, to surrender, and give up every story?

Surrender is giving up everything that I try to tell myself about the way life is. There is nothing that I can describe, that I think of, that I can feel, that I can know, that is accurate. So I surrender all of those faculties. They are not working. They don't give the level of information that I need because they don't give me what is whole. They don't address the irritation. They don't address the basic cycle of conflict.

Surrender means annihilation and descent into the heart. We live in a conceptual world in our head in which all worlds are created. But the world of actuality is not in the head. It's not conceptual, although it can utilize the conceptual. It can use the thoughts, the feelings, and the basic apprehension of the physical world. But it does not reside in an individual sense; the actual is non-located. We use the metaphor of the heart for the actuality of interconnectedness, so think of it as a heart attack. The descent into the heart breaks up all structures.

When we try to perceive the actual, our mind wants to understand it, to control and direct it. This is the fundamental illusion that we have to surrender: the idea that we're going to find actuality, organize it, and use it. We can't find the actual, we can't describe it, we can't do anything with it. The possibility of intelligence comes from that which remains when we give up everything we know.

This is not an evolutionary and passive process. Something active is moving, and the only action that is left is surrender. It is not passive. The passive response is a trick of the conceptual mind, which suggests that surrender is just giving up my inclinations. The *me* weaves its story of surrender to itself. I'm not really giving up. I'm giving up to a new story that I've created.

There is only one true action, the final surrender.

It is an action, not a choice, in the same way that when your knee is hit, your foot goes up. When you see that there's no other action to take, that's the reflex, the action that's left. When you see that there are lots of choices to make, there is a search, there is progress, there's management, then that is where that active force will go and be dissipated into distraction. When that distraction is no longer of interest, it doesn't draw you. Then the reflex, the action, is surrender.

What remains, then, is what forms our life. And there is very little that we can say about that, because what we know about is the other world of distraction, of separation, of conflict. So if you want to speak of that, if you want to utilize this old brain to form concepts and metaphors about it, then you will have to dive in to the unknown. It may not even be expressed in that old brain. It may express in some new way that we are discovering.

What do you actually know when you're in the unknown? Where is your body sense? Can you apprehend that now? Can you surrender everything you know, every bit of your history? If you surrender everything that you know, then what do you know that is not simply your concept?

Surrender is all that you can actually do. It's the only action any of us can actually take. All other actions are ideas.

Actuality resides in the unknown. We just don't know anything about it, because that with which we know constructs a personal reality. And we see that personal reality is not accurate.

We have spent our whole life creating our story and we don't want to let go of it.

Can you give up every story within the story, within *that* story, and within *that* story—every explanation, every philosophy, every getting better—the sum total of which is fear? Fear is the nature of the personal self. You can hold that fear together, which is a mechanical and conditioned unfolding, or you can surrender, which is the one true action available to us.

The only thing we know about death is the moment when the whole fear construct falls away and then arises again and the shock of *me-ness* occurs. If we really pay attention to it, we will see that *me* is fear.

This moment and the death process are the same. You will always meet death here. Here is always the opportunity to surrender and to experience something that you don't know about. The relief of death is the relief from living in fear, the relief from the burden of the known. That is available here. Right now. And it will always be. And the one opportunity to take the one action that you can take will always be here and now. That is to surrender to what is.

It's not an action that you take. It's simply an action. What we think of as our action is the mechanical nature of the thought process. That is passive. Those actions are just the conditioned mind at work. We have no authorship of those so-called actions because there is no author. Surrender is the action that is the active principle, not my action; surrender is not even in the repertoire of the conceptual mind. It is the active principle of life.

If you give up—totally surrender the mechanical process that you think of as the actor, as the self—if you see its complete bankruptcy, its lack of utility, then what's left? There is a reflex that comes from life itself, which is action. It is only one action, and it takes place in the presence of this moment.

Presence is not inert. Silence is not stillness. It is action. These are words. Find out in your life.

SURRENDER
TO WHAT?

ALL DESCRIPTIONS ARE INACCURATE, INCLUDING THIS ONE. ANY story we have is a distortion. Any meaning, any location, any placement in time is approximate, subjective, constructed in a relative reality. These are the deceptions of the self: that I can locate life in a place, in a sequence, and describe it accurately; that I know where I am and where you are and the meaning of all the components we describe.

We've developed spirituality around these concepts, and that spirituality has been co-opted into the religion of commercialism. In recent magazines you will find a full-page advertisement with a fine looking cup of coffee in the midst of what looks like a Zen rock garden. The text reads, *Some meditate for hours searching for inner peace. Others find it instantly: Serenity, tranquillity, balance. It's all right here, made fresh in your cup. Rich, smooth, Taster's Choice™.*

This is what we've collectively created out of the whole inquiry into the nature of life. A cup of Taster's Choice coffee.

This is of course what we create in ourselves as well—spiritual enlightenment as a commodity. Enlightenment is a cup of something that's going to get us a reward. We're quite active in attempting to create, to construct, this enlightened state to get the cup of something. At some point that neurotic activity breaks down and we're left with our one true action as a doer, that is, surrender. Give up the whole attempt to characterize life, to control life, to locate yourself, to sequence yourself in time. Serenity, tranquility, balance will have to come in our cup of coffee, or as a gift of the universe, not as the promised result of our contorted asanas, our awareness meditation, or our endless attempts at doing nothing.

We try to surrender to something, but there is no finish to the sentence, *Surrender to....* We find a teacher. Let's surrender to the teacher. We find a system. Let's surrender to that— a meditation, an experience, a woman, a man, whatever it is. We surrender to those things until we don't have anything left to surrender to. And then we just surrender to... it doesn't have anything attached to it. There is no promise. There is no result. There's nothing. That *surrender to...* is the quality we can call the quantum reality. It is not to an object, a thing, a process, a result, even a fine cup of coffee. It's not surrender to anything in particular. It is the surrender to everything, to the actuality of life just as it occurs, and the surrender to the unlimited potential of the quantum reality, to what is next.

It's the surrender of the notion of surrendering. As we do it, we give up even that. Otherwise surrendering becomes an identity, a badge of spiritual honor, the idea that *I'm a surrendered person now; I just accept everything as it is.*

Surrender is fresh in each moment and requires the full contact of our life to potentiate what is next.

It's not a method. It's not a philosophy. It's not a teacher. It's not anything like that. The conditioned mind wants nothing to do with actual surrender. So what could possibly activate the action?

It's the collapse of the known, the collapse of the effort, the exhaustion of any attempt to get anywhere, and the final action, the surrender to... The rest of the sentence is unfinished, because it has collapsed into itself, and now something else is possible. Anything else is possible. We've left the world of form and, as we pass through the formless, the alchemical shift reveals form as energy and the creation of what is next.

In that moment, we don't stay in that world of formlessness. We return to form. In the moment that the black hole collapses into itself, it begins to create the new universe. We're not leaving form. This is where we may make the fundamental error of thinking that we find a state that is beyond form, beyond me, that is surrender to...and now I'm done. I'm in some place that is transformed. It's not transformed, because it has to return to form. It has to move back into and through the same reality that we thought we just left. I have to be me again.

Something may have happened, but it's not in the world of form, it's not in the world of time. It's not knowable.

It isn't a change, because nothing is going to happen to you, nor could anything happen to you. So what's the point of the surrender? That phrase *surrender to...* didn't have an asterisk with a little footnote that describes the purpose of surrendering. Spirituality has a point to it. There's a reason for spirituality. But we have left spirituality. There is no point in surrendering, no goal, no object; it is the last action remaining, and it occurs as an authentic expression of the exhaustion of all other possibilities.

When we look for a reason for our surrender, we have to ask ourselves from what vantage point we view that reason. We have to sit in a place to observe, and that will characterize what occurs. Even if we expand ourselves into God's eye and try to understand it from God's eye, that isn't big enough. Whatever the vantage point is, it is a restriction.

From the perspective of the self we've entered into a terrifying place, a total tantric reality. We have plunged into the very energies that we've been running from all this time. Now not only are we back to those qualities again, but we are them. There is no separation. The fear is fear and the ecstasy is ecstasy. That wasn't exactly what we signed up for; we wanted to have a little controlled ecstasy and keep the fear away. But now life is precisely as it is, energetic in its quality. Without even so much as resting in the moment we have so long cultivated, life is creating what is next. We can't stand back from it. We can't characterize it. We can't divide ourselves from it. We can't control it. We can't protect ourselves from it.

We are without perspective. Where we have formerly spent so much energy sorting our experiences, there is simply the energy of life expressing itself through form as an aqualitative energy. Aqualitative means we are without the characterization of good or bad, like or dislike—without the distinction of qualities we subjectively assign. We're now also amoral. We have left the world of ethics and morality for an acausal, amoral, and aqualitative world. This is how dangerous it is.

It's the verb *to be*. It's an action, but it's an action that is outside of time. It is not action in the way that we have understood action; it is the impersonal acting through the personal with its own intelligence that supersedes our capacity to mediate, understand, or make traditional moral sense. And it's not a quality in the way that we've understood quality; we may like or dislike, but this is irrelevant to the energy. It is not located. It's not the *me* that's having that energetic movement. That's life, in which the self happens to be placed, but self is not at the center of it.

In our life, in our actual moral and immoral acts, there's absolute responsibility. Remember, we are life. It is not just a person taking an immoral action against another. We are the entire context. We are the actor and the receiver of that action.

It's far worse than we imagined. We thought we were going to get out of responsibility because it is the universe doing it, not me. Before at least we were able to pin responsibility on someone else: my mother, my father, God, samsara, karma, genes, something! Something else is responsible for the way I am, because I certainly don't like the way I am. But when I leave the realm of like or dislike, I am the way I am. And the way that I am is the expression of totality. How can you not be responsible for that? There is no one else left to be responsible.

I can only say that action came from me. This is life. This is my life. This is who I am. I am life. There is no way out.

When we talk about our experience of life, we refer to self-defining fragments. We talk about them as if they were the totality. Do the reverse. Go into the totality and then talk about fragmentation. Can you find the totality in this moment and create words from it? Can you find the total sense of connection and take that into words, into a symbolic representation?

This is the nature of dialog. It takes place when we're talking with each other from a shared, open space. The language that comes out is infused with that totality. Dialog is not a debate. It's not a philosophical discussion. And so it goes directly into our lives. Dialog means relationship, contact, and community. It means deep feeling with no escape. If dialog is anything, it is the expression of wholeness moving through reality, each of us engaged with the other.

The brilliance of wholeness is that it does innately express itself; it even expresses the inability to express. The expression may be silence. It may even be, on rare occasion, philosophical discussion.

Communication that grows out of this transformation can take all kinds of forms. Language is one of them. Perhaps in the past we were using words to try to get to something by finding their etymological source and being legalistic about what they mean. This approach suggests that words have innate meaning, rather than what seems more obvious—that the meaning itself is created in the dialog of speaker and listener, writer and reader. Meaning that is created in the moment also dies in the moment. That spontaneous, poetic expression, be it words or anything else, is a reflection of the apprehended whole.

We become actors in this vastness, because this vastness is moving through us and its demands take us beyond our capacity. The quantum reality is that anything could express through you. You could be the things that you think you aren't. Then again, you might not be the things you think you are. You could be anything, but anything is still ordinary.

The marvelous is ordinary in that sense. The world of synergy and coincidence, the synthesis of reality into something new, is all miraculous.

The capacity in our life is always going to be taxed. Whatever we are doing, there is always going to be more. Whatever we are not doing, there is always going to be less. That's how we're being utilized. That's what the flow of quantum reality is like. We can't possibly know anything about it because every boundary we get to, life expands beyond it. Every time I say this is all I can do, there is more required. And when I say this is the deepest feeling I've ever had, it gets deeper. Every form that we never thought would occur in our lives is occurring. We find ourselves living with people who are completely incompatible with us. We find ourselves in workplaces or in life situations that are unmanageable. Our lives possess the oddest collection of attributes.

That's beautiful, as long as we surrender to... When we resist, that unmanageability flattens us.

We want to present ourselves in the way we want to be seen, primarily to ourselves, but also to everyone else. We try to manage our lives to avoid exposing ourselves the way we are, actually. Which is scarier: not managing our lives, which is about as scary as it gets, or managing our lives and never having any actual contact with anything, never having a real relationship with anyone, never being swept away by feeling, whether it is passion or angst? Choose your fear.

We convince ourselves that if we manage our lives, the future will be rosy and happy. This is like going to the palm reader over and over again. She keeps saying, you're going to meet a tall, dark, handsome stranger. And you come back a year later and say, "I haven't met him yet." So she says, "This year you're going to. That'll be another fifty bucks." At some point you don't go to the palm reader anymore.

Do we see enough of the management pattern yet to see that it is not bringing us anything but a disconnected world? If we do see that, then we can allow the management to cease right now. Our whole life will crumble, and then we'll wake up in that same moment, with that same life, without a management plan.

There is something intelligent and alive in us that automatically switches into a self-centered perspective when needed. We are completely self-centered when crossing the street. We might even take the role of being self-centered on behalf of our children, because they may be in a non-located reality when crossing the street. Even in the deranged form of self-centeredness, we don't have to manage it, because neurosis actually has information in it. When I become neurotic in relationship, it tells me that relationship is bound somehow by some idea. It is not entirely free. And it's reflecting itself in this kind of neurotic pattern. Without the neurotic pattern I wouldn't know that. If I was just non-dual and believed everything is fine the way it is, then that contact wouldn't take place.

All energies of life, all qualities of life, are an expression of life itself. They have the movement that is required imbedded in them. It is not just the acceptance of life as it is, but the acceptance of life as it is while in full contact with it and with the emergence of what is next. It's not just transcendent. It's transcendent and transformational.

Nothing happens. Nothing changes. Nothing about our life is different. We're in the same life.

The function of the spiritual journey is to give it up, isn't it? So let us do that. Why wait? The experiment in life is not the spiritual journey. It is the expression of this energetic reality. Find the fact, the actuality of this present moment in your being, and the creation of what is next. It is not mediated by anybody in particular. That's what is beautiful about it. It doesn't travel hierarchically, conceptually, through time and process. The energy of life exists as a quantum reality with the full potential for anything. Try to conceptualize that—at this moment, any possibility, any form, any expression, without time or location, can occur. You can see that the thinking process, the conceptual mind, is completely incapable of handling this. Now you can try, if you like, and please do so if you're not satisfied that the conceptual mind doesn't function in this quantum realm whatsoever. This realm functions, if it would like, as the conceptual mind. But the conceptual mind doesn't control, does not encompass, does not measure this realm at all. So the quantum reality—what is next—is not knowable. It's not going to be captured by our philosophies, our religions, or our spirituality.

We may feel that we need to reside in a non-thinking realm, that we need to shift our obsession with the conceptual mind to a focus on non-locality, and that this is the crux of our transformation.

It's only the beginning. There is no end-point. There is only what is next. That is what is lovely about life; we're never going to come to a conclusion. We can only come to the beginning.

It's not so much a shift in focus as it is a recognition of what has been the fact all along. Haven't you always been this? Satori is not a discovery of something new. Satori is the discovery of something that is already.

It has nothing to do with thinking or non-thinking. Both are in this quantum reality. All expressions are in the possibility of the quantum reality. The quantum reality doesn't have an outside and an inside, a good and a bad. It has *what is next* as its characterization. It has every possibility, and this is why it's hard for the thinking mind, which is so used to distinctions, categorizing, sorting into liking and disliking.

Any "doing" by the thinking mind to comprehend this is useless. And from the quantum reality, the notion of non-doing is equally ridiculous. The quantum reality is dynamically creative. And if quantum reality were to have jokes, probably one of the jokes would be the idea of not doing, which we take so seriously. Some people even write books about such things, with titles like *Doing Nothing*.

CAN WE INVITE EVERYTHING
INTO OUR LIVES?

We CANNOT CONCEPTUALIZE MORE THAN A SAMPLE OF TOTALITY. Thought is an aspect and can never apprehend the whole. Is there any way to get to the whole? Are we endlessly representing in thought something that we cannot get to? We've taken the one action that we can take, which is surrender. Now we are out of actions to take. The fires of transformation are crackling, burning something, and creating some kind of side effect. Is this the only thing we can really know about the fires—the resistance and the breakdown into something else? What happens in that surrender?

I might discover that I am the totality. Now I am That. But I still argue with my wife. I still have trouble with my children. I am mad at my boss. I am getting old. Life is passing me by even though I am life! But I still wonder...

I've taken the paradox, contradiction, and confusion and answered that question with my cleverness. Consciousness is All. We are One. I know that the knowing is false. I've got both sides covered. If you're betting on the World Series and you bet on both teams, you're covered. If you buy a stock long and short, you're covered. If you have a wife and a girlfriend, well, you're covered and you're in deep trouble. We try to cover ourselves with this cleverness. Is that it? We're done?

What about conflict, war, disease, justice, poverty, pain? Is that still there?

What happens when you meet me and I'm in pain? My life's a mess. Since you're a surrendered person, what is your message to me? What shall I do about the confusion in my relationships? What do I do about my children, my money woes, my pressures, my mind that says to me every single day that I'm not enough? Or my mother says this to me when we talk.

Let me up the ante. There's a tumor growing in my body. What about that? Is that just my mind? It's hitting nerves and there is constant pain. It's clear to me I'm dying. Is that in the mind?

Are you going to go there to find out? Are you willing to experience that in your body? Is the thing we call compassion an idea that we use so we don't actually experience our connection, not just to the bubbly happiness, but to the deep pain? Maybe it is true that it all is mind. But how do we find that out unless we plunge into it? Are we distancing ourselves, not only from our own life, our own conflicts, but from the conflicts and the pain in life around us, saying, well, it's all mind, and I feel compassion for the pain of that illusion, as if that somehow addresses it?

Neuroscientists describe mirror neurons that are designed to generate our actions and to reproduce the sensation of the actions of those we observe as if we were taking the action. Whether they are creating the action or taking in the action of another, the mirror neurons fire in the same manner. We have the ability to embody what we see in the other. There is speculation among the neuroscientists that this is the basis for empathy and compassion, but it is also seen as an effective tool for prediction and survival. In our capacity to embody the other, what do we construct around this experience? Is it the profound empathy of their condition, an experience of being one? Is it the decoding of the other's intentions so that we can protect ourselves, attack more effectively, or get to resources more agilely than they? On the neuron level it is both the unraveling of the other's intentions and the deep feeling of what that is within our own system.

Maneuvering for a desirable outcome puts me in a privileged position. Only good things should happen to me. The very structure of me—all my ideas—is the addiction to separation and the fear of totality. It's a way of trying to contain the out-of-control nature of actuality—out-of control in the sense that it's out of my control. And if it is out of my control then it is clearly dangerous.

Actuality could be mega-desirable. It could be the opposite. It could be anything. It could be beyond description. So this is the question, oh, explorers of reality. Are you really explorers or are you armchair readers, voyeurs, travel channel watchers? This is the question, because it does take your life. That is the price, your life. That's what the fire needs to burn—you. Surrender is accepting that life is unknown. Even the messiness is unknown. I thought I was going to find a way to fix that, contain it, segment it, control it, transcend it. But now I don't even know if it is messy. When your life becomes a question, it changes the nature of the conflict. It is only by my definition, and where I want to be, and what I want, that the conflict is there.

Now conflict becomes something else. It is energetic. It is moving and changing something. It is transformative. The relative reality becomes something else, not something we're fighting. It is the embodiment of totality. It is the expression of the very thing we say we want. If we stop involving ourselves with the manipulation of our own description, we may see that. Once seeing it, there's no way back.

Totality is everything that is happening in your own body/mind and everything that is *not* happening in your body/mind. Embodiment is the only thing that we can find. That's why trying to fix the universe by what we know is ludicrous, because what we don't know is constantly folding into the known. This is what manifestation is. We become enamored with the manifestation, forgetting that it is already gone and that what is next, which is the unknown, is now expressing. All we can see is the known—a ghost image that has nothing to do with what is next.

So, in coming to the end of the spiritual search, we actually come to the beginning of the exploration of consciousness. This is not a path of looking or finding; it is not negating the thought process or changing anything. It is the exploration of the manifestation and embodiment of totality, which is expressing itself in what is next after now, in my body, in my life, in my relationship, in all the forms and expressions that are apparent and all the forms and expressions that are not.

We step away from the ideals and step into a fluid reality. This can be a scary world because it means that we don't control the passions, the dark energies, all the things that we've learned to control. There is no guarantee that we will become loving, kind, or anything else; we may plunge into the opposite. Compassion, when it arises in us, doesn't present a particular challenge. It is when the unacceptable forms rise up in us that we are challenged with fear. But is it actually fear that we experience in the face of the actual? The way that we always understand the phenomenology of our experience is in relation to me. But what is fear if there is no fearer? Universal fear—the fear that exists as an energy—is that differentiated from love? Are we ready to invite in totality? That could look like anything. It's not just cool. It's not just cerebral. It's not just in control. It's not just hot, out-of-control, or moving either.

We are back at the beginning, which is the end, and we have no guide. There is no teacher, no form, no philosophy, and no structure, that can help here. And in fact, none is needed. Because totality itself is expressing itself right in front of us. Can we invite everything into our lives?

SURVIVAL

THINKING MAKES PREDICTIONS BASED ON MEMORY AND MY DESIRE to survive, and for that it is an exceedingly good tool. But it doesn't work for *our* survival. That is a different faculty. If a transformation happens, it is from "How do *I* survive?" to "How do *we* survive?"

Thought is mechanical. It does not have any particular independence. It just is what it is. And it suggests within itself all kinds of universes, including its own substantiality. In thought's projection of a subject-object world I need to protect myself from you and I need to accumulate certain levels of status and materiality. But there is actually nothing to get or to protect at a seminar on spirituality, at a university, or at Wal-Mart. The whole idea of acquisition is based on the fiction of the acquirer. Who is it that is accumulating?

Go to the root of that question—there is no one there. There is just the movement of thought suggesting a *me* and driving all the wanting. There is no recognition, there's no recognizer, there's nothing to be recognized, there is just what is—not a fixed state, but an energetic movement that embodies thought but is not generated by thought. This is a simultaneous multiplicity of states that are energetically and materially entangled. Rather than this or that, it's this *and* that.

We are all encased in realities that we think are so substantial, and we go through the dramas and the stresses of our reality on a daily basis, until something occurs that breaks through that reality. If you are a policeman holding a gun on somebody who is robbing a bank, then within that reality that is what you do and that is what you are, just as the robber is a robber in his construction. If someone taps you on the shoulder and zaps you with some new understanding, you might drop your gun, take off your uniform and go sit in a lotus position somewhere. But until that occurs, you are still a policeman.

Reality shifts without reason or warning. That can be a tragedy, a death, a sickness, a failure. The crack in reality is the opening to what is beyond, and if it is not filled with a new set of beliefs, then this openness simply remains unformed and available to what is next.

Language creates the show of reality. Language is the extension of biological survival instincts. The body suggests that it lives apart from all other bodies and that we should take survival-oriented actions. But from the Gaian perspective, my body doesn't make any difference, nor does yours. We are future compost, regardless of the size of our bank accounts, the glory of our careers, or the success of our children. We are delivery systems for bacteria and viruses, and carriers of genes. If you look at it from the broadest perspective, the whole contrivance of survival is absurd. Without the cultural construction of time, we are not even blips. We function as if we are something, because we think we are surviving by doing that. Ironically, as we extend this egoic logic, we are collectively destroying ourselves.

When we see that the objective world doesn't exist in separation, then we are left with a world in which what we see is what we are. We are also left with a world where the conflicts we experience in the subject-object world are still there. While we recognize that what we see is what we are, there is still going to be an argument with the husband or the wife, there are still wars going on in the world. What is the ramification of the realization that the war is me? That the dispute with my wife is me? When I see that the illness manifesting in my body is me? When the whole thing becomes a unitary experience, it brings us back to an energetic reality. Now we can only go into it, rather than distance ourselves from it.

Here's a challenge. Try to go through one day, one twenty-four-hour period, where you relate to the world as if what you see is what you are. The people that you don't like are what you are. The people that you do like are what you are. Your conceptual world will collapse. Belief is essential to the structure of self and it is the reality in which we spend our time. Yet even without these judgments functioning is still going on, it is just not taking place through some kind of volitional movement. The construction of judgment suggests to us that there is a deciding process that we are operating, but in actuality this deciding is occurring prior to our construction.

There is nothing wrong with the conceptual, it's just that we have taken the conceptual to be the universal, and it is not. One of the big delusions in the spiritual world is that we are going to do away with thought. You'd have to hit your head with a sledgehammer, have a major car accident, or overdose on drugs to get rid of thought. You could wipe out your conceptual capacity, but why would you want to? Transformation has nothing to do with doing away with thought. If anything, sharpen your thought. Be the most brilliant thinker there is and understand what thought is.

PART 2

BREAKTHROUGH

POST-SPIRITUALITY
AND ACTUALITY

Human beings are part of a whole called by us the "Universe," a part limited in time and space. We experience ourselves, our thoughts and feelings, as something separated from the rest—a kind of optical delusion of consciousness. This delusion is a kind of prison for us, restricting us to our personal desires and to affection for a few persons nearest us. Our task must be to free ourselves from this prison by widening our circles of compassion to embrace all living creatures and the whole of nature in its beauty.

—Albert Einstein

SUBLIME
CONFUSION

IF WE HAVE COME TO THE END OF THE MASTERS AND GURUS, THE RELI-gions and philosophies, the process of getting better and achieving, we have stepped into a condition that is entirely unknown. What is it that I am? There is no longer a narrative to explain the experiences of our life, no longer a story that weaves our life together to give us a sense of time, location, and meaning. This is an essentially negative space in which we have deconstructed everything we know, including the purpose and meaning of the deconstruction.

This negative space is a relatively powerful one in that it can destroy any construction. It is vigilant to any attempt to create, undermining anything that is positive or idealistic. But once it has destroyed all that is false in our lives, all the conceptualizations that make up our individuated reality, there is nothing left for it, just as there is nothing left of our lives other than the bare functioning.

Many of us would recognize this space as depression, depersonalization, and disconnection. Spiritually defined, it might be known as detached. Religiously, it is the dark night of the soul. We are devoid of the false, but we are also devoid of the truth. That movement of negation, having consumed the positive, begins to consume itself, like the snake swallowing its own tail.

This ultimate and pristinely pure state is without even the solace of deconstruction because the negative has negated itself. There is neither illusion nor is there clarity. The world of opposites ends. Understanding becomes confusion, subtle in its qualities, but fundamentally without discrimination in anything other than the relative and concrete world of the day-to-day functioning. Any attempt to extrapolate from the immediate and practical reality that presents itself can only be a swirl of undefined movement.

Sublime confusion is our failure to comprehend the world, yet it is our synthesis of the pointlessness of understanding as an abstraction. It is the breakout into a relationship to the world which is not mediated by understanding of any recognizable kind, yet it is a deep understanding of unknowing.

Any attempt to concretize this fluid state is futile—and confusing.

What is sublime in this confusion is the liberation from the weight of knowing, the defended positioning, the aggression of point of view. We are trained from an early age to occupy a place of knowing, yet we know that we do not know. We are imposters in our own life, and this undermines the natural creativity, replacing it with an actor pretending to achieve, to relate, to exist. What is sublime is the sweetness of foolishness, the openness of fresh contact with a world that makes no sense, that is without explanation, that is without cause.

Sublime confusion is what occurs when we are cracked open so thoroughly that, like the meaning of the word *confusion,* we move from form to form without resistance. This is what life appears to be, the movement of form to form, dynamic, fluid, and without center or periphery, itself unknowing until the creative expression of what is next.

POST-SPIRITUALITY

IF WE HAVE GIVEN UP SPIRITUALITY, NOT AS A REACTION AND NOT AS a completion of some mythic journey, but more precisely as a vaporization of the contrivance that it represents, we are left in a post-spiritual reality. In the post-spiritual condition, then, there is no longer reference to the construction of spirituality, other than as a historic reference, much like a reference to the weather last year, which occurred but has no specific reflection in our life today.

Even the notion of post-spiritual needs to be abandoned if we are to discover what is next. All concepts create the appearance of a substantial reality but in actuality are insubstantial.

This negation is not simply a philosophical or semantic twist, rather the liberation that spirituality promised but could never deliver. No philosophy or system of thought, no belief system or religious perspective can deliver the absolute freedom that is already present and always will be.

The great liberation is actual and requires nothing, gives nothing, contains nothing, and creates nothing. We are all done, whether we like it or not, whether we are spiritual or not, whether we agree with this or not. When we cease to characterize life as a process with attendant goals, we apprehend what has always been the case, an acausal world in which manifestation is absolutely true and description is relatively not. The actual is, the conceptual is not, other than within itself. The conceptual is always reflective and fragmented, never actual and complete. As such, concept is useless in contacting actuality.

The great liberation then is not a state, but an energetic manifestation, an actuality, not an idea. We could say that this energy is manifest in each of us, if there were an each of us, rather than an all of us. We could say this energy is all of us, if there were any of us, rather than none of us, in the actual. We can find an each, an any, an all of us in the relative world of ideas and in the somatic world of bodies and brains. But in the post-conceptual we know that these are relative worlds and that the energy manifestation, the actual, is not each of us, all of us, or any of us, because we are not.

It is not a negative world though; there is something, not nothing, in the world, and even though it is not defined by a me or an us—despite our churning thought worlds that suggest this—the world is full and manifest.

The inquiry is not spiritual, because there is no entity to become, but there is an inquiry nonetheless. The manifest world—the actual—is dynamic, and the inquiry is intrinsic to its direction and creation. As quantum physics shows, phenomena are altered by observation. Observation is a kind of creative force suggesting that the flow of consciousness through the actual is both the transformation and the manifestation.

It is entirely without a me, without a center located in space and embedded in time, that we explore the energetic flow of the quantum reality. The inquiry is left completely in the manifestation; we can only explore what is actual. The actual moment is not now; now is dead and past, a spiritual invention of the purveyors of tranquility and enlightenment. The actuality is what is next after now, not in time, but in the manifestation of the directional stream of conscious energy that we are.

We are always poised on the edge of creation, but we can only think about it in time, referencing the past and deluding our perspective with continuity. We cannot create from the unknown, we can only replicate what is past, and this replication is itself still conceptual.

The actual does not reference anything, it does not come from anything, it has no future. It is the very expression of what is next, unpredicted by any means that are known.

We have accepted the indoctrination of the power of now, but now has no power, even for those who grow rich selling it. The power lies in what is next after now—what creates and destroys exists there, not here. Here, in the now, we are stuck, holding on, hoping this is it, hoping we can finally rest like the speakers and the writers, the saints and mystics have told us— here and now. The actual is neither here nor now; there is no rest, and there is no one to be resting. The actual universe is dynamic *and* still, and now is only still—the stillness already smashed by what is next.

Now is corrupted by the stories with which we have filled it. We can purify the moment by leaving it; it never was, as it turns out. Only what is next is actual—it is the manifest, and in a world stripped of ideas, there is only manifestation.

We thought we were freed from the past and the future when we discovered the timeless present, but we were only imprisoned in one more idea. Concepts divide, and the now is a concept. Live in the now and you die, because you live in the now. Die in the now and you die to the now, reborn entirely refreshed in what is next. Incarnation is the failure to recognize reincarnation as essential truth, endless without time, endless without location or persona. Birth is the denial of life, and death is the embrace of immortality. What is next is all that there is, and it creates birth and death as equals.

Is there a way to stop the thought process and to perceive in a new way? Thought creates a sense of self, a central organizing principal, which appears separate and in conflict. This same self, which is a creation of thought, then thinks it will resolve this conflict by thinking. All the efforts of the thinking mind to extract itself from thought are entirely useless. Thought can only move in its own field—of more thought. Doing nothing about the thinking mind is the recognition that thought is not an area where what is new will be discovered. In this respect, all of our philosophies, spirituality, and religion can be abandoned, as well as any effort to improve. The monk who has meditated for fifty years and the average person on the street are essentially the same, although their behaviors may be relatively different. All of us are functioning within the framework of the conceptual world, whether it is the idea of working for money or working for enlightenment.

We don't need to stop meditating, reading spiritual books, or going to spiritual events any more than we need to stop going to movies, reading novels, or having coffee at a café. These are all expressions of life. But let us not be under any illusion that meditation is different from a movie or that meeting with teachers is different from reading a fantasy novel. If we enjoy this kind of entertainment, that is fine. Is there a way to engage in life without a strategy, without it being framed in some enlightenment myth or improvement game?

There is no escape from the conceptual world, simply because it doesn't have any independent existence. No existence, no escape. We expend our life dealing with the nonexistent self in its nonexistent world, a self that is running from its fear of nonexistence. If we stop running we will be consumed by this fear, which of course is not fear, but the fact of nonexistence. What is there then? Not something else; there is everything else.

In the deconstruction of our conceptual framework—that is, in seeing through the elements of time, location, and meaning—we are left with the actual, the "everything else." Everything is a lot, certainly more than we bargained for when we began searching for our enlightenment. Everything is obviously and bluntly more than our capacity, however grand our spiritual experiences are, however long we sit in meditation, regardless of how many teachers we have collected. The actuality of life, the all and everything, introduces us to total confusion, sublime confusion, the overload of our capacity to understand. We can run from this confusion back to an explanation, a philosophy, a system of some kind to organize and to give meaning and process to our life. Or, we might recognize the disorganization of our understanding as a doorway through which to enter an actual life, a life that has dimensions entirely unknown to us.

It is not that the world is an illusion; it is, in fact, unknown. What is the illusion is the conceptual knower and its grand illusion, the known. We occupy ourselves with organizing and expounding our certainties without ever questioning the basis of our knowledge. If we confront the basics of our conceptual world—time, location, and meaning—we may notice that whatever is operating is doing so without these elements. Try to have certainty without the movement of past to future, without a subject-object relationship, and without the description of experience.

The fact is most of us will seek teachers, books, and groups for guidance. Most of us will take up practices of spiritual technology to improve our chances of happiness, fulfillment, or the mythic enlightenment. In that process, we will accumulate more clutter of concepts and experiences, subtler and less accessible versions of the idea of self. We will blunt the extreme pain we started with, the pain of separation that drove us to seek solutions. We will learn how to stay calm, how to be spacious. We will be sold awareness like it is a new car. Here is how to be aware, then how to be more aware; soon we will learn how to be really, really aware. And the narrative that runs through all of this is that if we can just be as aware as the teacher, or the Buddha, or some other spiritual ideal, then we will be free of pain and always happy and get to sit in the chair in the front of the room and tell others all about it. This is a fairy tale.

Life is delivering the truth to each of us in each moment without need for anyone to mediate it. Pain is the resistance to the movement of the life energy, and it is the expression of that movement.

If we happen upon someone who is exploring the movement of life and have the deep feeling to enter into relationship to that person and to that exploration, then of course we will do so. This is a relationship without requirement. We do not need to construct anything around that relationship other than to live in it with the deepest integrity, and we will certainly get absolutely nothing from it. This nothing is love.

It is not that we cannot do anything; we are doing something all the time, but what is it we are doing? We are already expressing confusion in our day-to-day lives; it is not the result of some realization. While we may constantly try to create a linear and causal sequence, such as *we should stop doing, then there will be confusion, then something else...*, we cannot discover causality other than in the idea of it. Without the idea of causality and the improvement that is suggested with this idea, what is our spirituality about?

Trust does not exist in the structure of mind, which is built entirely on survival—measuring the world by dividing it into subject and object and creating methods of moving through that created world to avoid death, whether physical or psychological. However, trust is the actual fact of life; it is really what we are left with when we see that these thought structures do not reflect life with any substantial accuracy and cannot guide us in any intelligent way. The totality of life is what is animating us, and recognizing this is a kind of trust that we cannot avoid even if we want to. And this unavoidable trust, despite every structure of our known world struggling against it, is the ultimate surrender to what is next.

WHAT'S
NEXT
AFTER NOW

T HROUGH ALL OF THE SPIRITUAL INDOCTRINATION, BENIGN OR manipulative, we became convinced that there was a kind of liberating experience in the moment. If we could simply force ourselves, surrender ourselves, or simply find ourselves consistently in the present moment, we would find passion or peace or whatever we were driven to acquire.

Unfortunately for our pursuit of liberation, there is nothing to find in the moment other than the projective capacity of mind. What is next after now eludes the mind entirely; it cannot be captured in this or any moment. Trying to be in the moment is a pointless exercise in futility. We obviously are in the moment to begin with, generating all kinds of conceptual realities, including the concept of a thoughtless mind. We have been sold on the moment, but the moment is no more alive than any other thought. What is truly alive is what is next.

What is next is a fluid intelligence, taking form but not holding the form beyond that singularity. This is a foreign quality from the perspective of the conceptual mind, which is entirely reliant upon the past and the rote repetition of historic phenomena. Fluid intelligence relies on destruction as much as creation; it creates acausally and spontaneously, smashing its creation simultaneously. This is quantum mind, not conceptual mind—higher only in the respect that it is intelligent and the conceptual mind is not.

We can understand the lack of intelligence of the conceptual mind easily enough—the fixed nature of a concept, the mimetic replication of thought, the quasi-religious quality with which we believe in the collection of ideas we carry around, even though they leave us with no flexibility in encountering life. It is true enough that these fixed templates we view life through give us the sense of location and stability, illusion though that may be. We do not need to discard such useful tools, nor can we anyway, but we can see their disutility. Fluid intelligence utilizes everything and believes in nothing.

The quantum mind expresses fluid intelligence as a tool to manifest and apprehend. Quantum mind holds all possibilities and all potentials unrestrained by the past or conditioned by any expectation of the future. This absolute freedom exists as an acausal energy, and while we may attempt to assign it the quality of a higher intelligence, it is intelligence unlike anything we can ideate. It is not the wrathful God of the Old Testament nor is it the loving God of the New Testament. It is neither a prophet nor a dispassionate observer.

The clues to the nature of this quantum mind are found in the subtle experiments and theories of quantum physics, in which the elemental energetic world is acting without predictability or pattern, other than the actual manifestation. Quantum physics suggests a mind-boggling universe so thoroughly entangled as to make the notion of discrete location meaningless.

Similarly, we can find hints in the unrelenting contact with each of our lives when we strip away the conceptual and reside in the actual. Without belief in concept, there is no causation, no meaning, no purpose.

At the core of the religious-spiritual search is the attempt of the fragmented center to find resolution, to transcend its own divided nature. The perspective from this center is impossible to resolve—the perspective itself obscures what is whole. The best that spirituality can offer is an experience of expansion, of peace, of connection. This is a lovely offering and it is accepted gladly by most of us. But imbedded in these experiences remains the perspective of the fragmented center, still clinging, still searching, still wanting.

The end of spirituality is simply the realization that the perspective that seeks resolution is the problem, and this cannot be solved, created as it is by the illusion of separation, which is thought itself.

Without the fragmented perspective that searches, there is no spirituality. The end of spirituality leaves the looking, without the looker. Post-spirituality is the perspective of the looking, a movement without an organizing center, without thought as the perspective. But this is not the absence of perspective, nor is it the absence of thought.

Spirituality has claimed a variety of omega points, places of meeting godhead, where the *me* touches transcendence. Post-spirituality recognizes nothing as the meeting point—the perspective is not from the fragment seeking the whole, but rather of the whole expressing as the fragment-in-the-whole.

Spirituality in all its forms, including non-duality, is dualistic; it is a fragment looking for unity. Post-spirituality is non-dualistic, evidenced by the reversal of perspective; the whole is expressing actuality. There is nothing to acquire, there is only the dynamic of creation-imbedded-in-destruction as an unknowable manifestation.

Spirituality has created the idea and the experience of the present, and with that creation has created the past and the future as equal but opposite ideas and experiences.

Post-spirituality does not concern itself with any division of time and does not care about maintaining contact with the present moment or any other constructed idea or experience. Post-spirituality is an expression of the quantum reality, which is timeless and therefore free to function in any experience of time or any non-experience of time. Time is a relative dimension and an expression of wholeness, like all relative dimensions.

In actuality, time is an experience constructed in thought, and the present is one of a multitude of such sub-constructions. The present is neither good nor bad. The past and future are neither good nor bad. Post-spirituality does not try to collect any particular construction or maintain any particular experience of time or timelessness.

Spirituality builds itself around self-location, the seeker who attempts to transcend, and the transcendent one who attempts to return to chopping wood and carrying cappuccino. Post-spirituality abandons the myths of self in all its forms and deals directly with the actual self, the manifest self just as it is, giving up all sense of improvement. The actual self is the precise manifestation of the whole.

Personal improvement is like sitting in a movie theater, arguing with the villain projected on the screen, and feeling wonderful that at least we have tried to make things better. We may feel connected to the character in the movie, but we are actually feeling connected to an idea; or most precisely, the feeling of connection is an idea.

Without time and location there can be no spirituality; without spirituality there is post-spirituality. Addicted to seeking and desperate for an identity, we may try to convert post-spirituality into something, even a not-something. But, what it is, simply, as the negative expression, is that it is, without *me*. As a positive expression, it is the actual, and actuality is a quantum reality, not a mechanical reality. The quantum reality is the potential for anything, unrestricted by any ideated past, present, or future.

Spirituality has no creative expression. As a conditioned expression of our sense of lack, it is caught in its own promise of fulfillment.

Post-spirituality is without promise; pain and pleasure are phenomenologically identical or aqualitative; fulfillment is a constructed experience; and there are no predictable structures to rely on. The post-spiritual life is entirely creative, because it lives in the unknown. Just as quantum physics has demonstrated the unpredictability of actuality, the post-spiritual sensibility is uncertainty, chaos, and confusion. This is a tremendously vital dynamic, reliant on no particular state, believing in no particular description, and moving as an expression of life.

ACTUALITY

WE OFTEN DISCUSS REALITY AS IF THIS IS AN OBJECTIVE, COMMON ground out of which we can build a coherent collective worldview. If we have come to see that reality, all reality, is conceptually based, then all reality is relative, including the one embedded in this sentence.

But, we hardly spend our lives pondering the nature of objective reality, and mostly we are occupied with thinking, emoting, doing, and some kind of sensate perception and reaction that we will leave to the brain researchers to sort out. Why should we be concerned with disassembling the subjective reality we construct in each moment, as if it is objective reality?

Indeed, the nature of subjective reality is to pose itself as objective reality. This allows us to be aghast at our opponents' actions, hurt by the words of our intimates, and to go through the drone of our daily lives as if there is clear meaning. To penetrate our notion of objective reality and discover it as subjective, then to worsen this appalling realization with the surprising insight that there is no subject to that relative reality is to take the risk that we will no longer function as we are used to.

A person could miss work, lose a marriage, and be considered entirely imbalanced simply by asking the basic question *Is the consensus reality actual?*

This question is different from asking how to best function within the constructed reality. After all, the best way to function is obvious: conceptually consider the relative, the constructed, to be objective and substantial. To function in the unreal we must convert it to reality. This is relative reality, but that will do.

But, should we happen upon the question of what is actual, not what is constructed reality, then the great unraveling occurs quite effortlessly. We cannot find any objective reality, only various levels of agreements, social constructions, personal constructions, and, on a small scale, we may even find brain/perceptual constructions.

We could look to science, which makes the auto-suggestion that it is objective, but science itself is a powerful belief system, so clearly seen as such when it is under siege by other powerful belief systems. Observe a creationist talk about intelligent design with an evolutionist defending Darwinism and you might see that passionate belief is a driving force of both camps.

Where can we find reality? We cannot conceptualize it without dropping inside the relative. We cannot perceive it without subjecting it to the approximating constructions of our body/mind, which does create the cognition of apparent reality, but not the apprehension of what is actual. We cannot feel reality energetically without the emotive conditioning that suggests a personal experience and all the attendant psychological history. In the end, we cannot find reality regardless of how hard we look, simply because that which looks is characterizing what it sees from the smallest elements of the quantum level to the macro level of archetype.

If through this unknowable nature, what we have named reality remains always relative, then it is not necessary to seek reality; we are already immersed in its veil of relativity. What stands outside the duality of relative reality is the actual. The actual is not reality and is not relative, nor is it the word *actual*.

The actual is not the source from which the word appears to come, or even what it appears to refer to. There is nothing in reality that the actual is. The actual does not have reality; it is the reality that reality is not. This purity comes with a price, which is that the actual has no relative quality, it has no division, no center and margin, no distinction, and cannot be relative to anything. The actual has no reality; it has no existence.

We can find reality in each moment. But, the actual can never be discovered, can never be known, can never be used. The actual is absolute, and our constructed reality is not. What the world is, is actual, what it is not, is reality. Yet, we live in reality, where we have existence, rather than in the actual, where we have none.

This assertion of our existence is like the logician's puzzle of ascertaining the veracity of the man who says, "Everything I say is a lie." If the man is telling the truth, then he must be lying. But, if he is lying, then he might be telling the truth, or telling part of the truth. As we consider the riddle, going deeper and deeper into its permutations, we become enamored with the puzzle and forget that there is no man, no lie, no truth, no logician. There are not even words on a page of a book. There is not even a brain constructing images. There is not even synaptic discharge, nor electromagnetic fluctuation in a biomass, nor a quantum fluctuation of energy. There is, in actuality, nothing knowable occurring; there is nonexistence and not the word or the concept *nonexistence,* so we cannot even say that there is nonexistence. We cannot say what there is. We can say that the actual is silent, unknowable, unspeakable, and it is coincidental with the manifestation of a tremendously complex, nested reality, which is not actual, but of the actual, in which we claim our existence. These are words and they are not it, they are a reality of opposites. The actual has no opposite and so has no reality, no existence, yet it is all that we are, all that we can have, all that we will ever be, in fact.

In the realm of reality we have so much to strive for, so much conflict, so much complexity. In actuality we have nothing, there is nothing to achieve, there is the simplicity of nonexistence.

Where we have the illusion of living is in reality, and where we appear to have nonexistence is in actuality, but where we have actual life is in what is next. We are neither the construction of the relative reality nor the nonexistence of the actual, but the crackling release of quantum potential, the fact of manifestation, the relentless energetic movement of becoming.

This quantum expression is the actual come alive, an acausal, aqualitative occurrence. If we are to live fully in this new actualism, we must first abandon any belief in reality as we have known it by abandoning belief itself, and our belief in belief is anchored in the superstition that the known tells us what is next. This belief in the known is reinforced because we reside in reality, which is known, and in reality, the known informs us what is next, because what is next is more of what we know. The belief in the known, the belief in belief, cannot step outside what it knows. Once outside the known, we must face that all of our beliefs and all of what we know tell us nothing at all about an acausal universe.

ACTUALISM
AND THE
RELEASE
OF
QUANTUM POTENTIAL

WE CAN DISCARD REALITY AS RELATIVE AND CONSTRUCTED. WE cannot have any experience of the actual; there is no non-constructed access to what is. Where we live is neither reality nor the actual, but the energetic expression of the actual as it manifests, without precedent, without future. We are the dynamic of actualism. While we will think and write of this as if it is a thing or a movement, it is not suspended between moments, nor is it bracketed by distinction, so it has neither the characteristics of a noun or a verb—neither thingness nor action. Our thinking of it cannot be accurate, although we will try to move actualistic occurrence into reality, where it is knowable, when actualism has no reality, only acausal becoming.

Can we step away from our archaic thinking and cease holding the vital actualism of our life in the containment of our created reality? We have understood creativity as a movement within reality, or perhaps a shift of reality, but actual creativity is a movement not based in reality at all. Access to this creativity is not an action; rather it is the release of the construction and an entry into a flow not directed by us. While this creativity does not originate in reality, it is the creator of the reality in which we suggest to ourselves that we are contained.

The possibility of creativity comes alive by the very fact that we must leave the known reality to enter the nonexistent actual, and it is in this purely energetic manifestation that creation occurs. Because it is a quantum energy without cause and without the structure of any precedent, anything can be created from this. Creating what is next includes all possibilities, not just repeating the past or modifying it. This unrestricted potential suggests that the New Age notion that *I create my reality* is very close to true, with one slight change, and that is to leave out the *I*.

Reality is created by the actual, and in that created relative reality there is the notion of a central *me*, which has built into it the sense that it exists, it creates, and it perceives reality. This relative reality, far from being real, is a manifestation, a side effect really, of the energetic discharge of the actual. The relative reality appears stable, but it is as insubstantial as the actual. There is good and bad news in this. The good news is that this fluidity allows immediate change; it is the basic fact of transformation or shift of reality. The bad news is that everything we think is real is gone in this moment and may or may not reoccur in what is next.

Clearly this is a challenge to our structure and stability and, at the same time, an amazing opening to creative flow. In perceiving this, we can see the release from the crushing weight of personality and past and the invitation to be, not as a passive voyeur of life, but as the energetic co-creator of always-new reality.

Can we think, feel, and act without the illusion of continuity and center? Is this an entirely new way to live, is it the old way without the stress, or is it just the same, neurosis and all? There is no answer to this in theory; the answer is found only in plunging into the life stream, which offers the madness of freedom and the ultimate responsibility of unity. The answer is not in words, but in what actually occurs and its spin-off in form, the manifestation of reality.

The quantum potential, the human potential, lies not in accessing deeper truths, or perfecting transactional skills, or perceiving new dimensions of reality, but rather in fully discovering the trans-actual, the oscillation of the actual and its manifestation of reality. This is not a personal or an impersonal discovery; it is the realization that we are the actual, and it is the actual that manifests. The impersonal is the quality of the actual, the personal the quality of reality, but it's the trans-actual that we are—both not personal and not impersonal.

We will have to set aside our personal development programs and our impersonal enlightenment in order to explore the trans-actual. We cannot get there from here; we can only get there from there. No psychological, spiritual, or religious process will be of any use and none of these processes will do any harm; they are all simply irrelevant. If we enjoy the reality of our quest and the company of teachers of the way, then, of course, we will continue to inhabit that virtual world. That reality is no closer or further from the actual than any other reality, so let's stay relaxed. But even if hubris has us in its grips and we are certain of our deep psychological needs, driven in our authentic spirituality, holier in our true religions, like it or not, we are no closer or further from the actual than the thieving drug addict, the oblivious shopping-addicted consumer, the addled television junkie. In an acausal universe where the actual manifests reality, we are all the manifestation of the transactual, we are all as close to the source as anyone else. The distance to nonexistence is nothing at all.

PART 3

BREAKOUT

CREATIVITY

Our deepest fear is not that we are inadequate. Our deepest fear is that we are powerful beyond measure. It is our light, not our darkness that most frightens us. We ask ourselves, "Who am I to be brilliant, gorgeous, talented, and fabulous?" Actually, who are you not to be? You are a child of the Universe. Your playing small does not serve the world.

—Nelson Mandela

THE
RISK
OF
CREATION

T HE SOURCE OF QUANTUM CREATIVITY IS NON-LOCATED; THAT IS TO say that it is located in the entirety. The creative utilizes the locus, utilizes time and space, but it is not of these qualities, certainly not limited to their boundaries. Actual creativity is not sourced from the *me* that we are so used to maintaining; rather it creates this locus.

That this is so disorienting to us results in an endless struggle to subsume what is beyond me into me, as if this activity had great meaning. We exert effort in an absurd attempt to reach from the created to the creative, as useless as suggesting that a sculpture struggle to chisel the sculptor. This effort leaves us with a sense of pressure and confusion, not creativity, but those qualities motivate a kind of agitation that we regard as creative. This neurosis activates us to do. And this doing agitates more neurosis. But doing is not creative; it is the byproduct of actual creativity.

Quantum creativity lies in dynamic communion that is both still and highly energetic. It can bring recognition and fame, and it can bring anonymity—creativity does not really care. We do care, however, and we try to guide it to name and fame, power and prestige, safety and security, or at least a modicum of happiness and a good story about our life. These are illusions of the temporal reality; the quantum creativity flows on without regard for these results. And when the fame becomes infamy, the name becomes notorious, the power leaks into oblivion, when the inevitable sickness and death occur, the quantum creativity has not stopped. It flows on.

Our potential is to discover ourselves as this quantum creativity, not as the conditions that are the side effects. In this human potential lies the undiscovered life.

Consider that the world of concept that we inhabit is secondhand—learned from teachers, mentors, and parents, perhaps culturally indoctrinated or biologically inherited. The template of thought that we place on every experience to measure it, to predict what is next, to survive the unknown, is a fixed form. There is nothing dynamic or creative about concept.

The first encounter, the first experience, the first glimpse without precedent has just a hint of the creative potential before it is entombed in memory. The conceptual efficiency of approximating the experience we are having by pulling from the past to assess the present and predict the future is a wonderful reality. Yet, concept as an approximating function is inaccurate. We are encountering all of our life for the first time each time, since each time is manifesting for the first time. We cannot know what the qualities of what is next actually are. We can live in the approximation of concept or step into the flow of the unknown.

The approximate world of concepts is mechanical, and—while it has little to do with the actual—as in an advanced computer game, we can be the hero, the warrior, the lover, the whatever, in the conceptual. Our life appears to be a creative theater piece unless we see that, like the computer game, the whole story is programmed, including our reflexive response.

Actual creativity is flowing; it has no back story and an uncertain future. We cannot conceptualize it, because there is no approximation of the unknown. No models apply. All that can possibly occur is new, and even if it is identical to what came before, what is next is always fresh.

Even as this sentence is being written and being read, there can be no knowing what meaning will be engendered by its words, what the non-coordinated collaboration among readers will create, what will be unfurled out of its framing of textualized reality. The risk of the creativity in these words is to write and to read, discovering, without knowing, what actually occurs.

We can look back and try to suggest a purpose, but we can't really know the purpose, because it is unfolding now and the implications are so vast. The instrument that we would use to measure it—our mind—isn't big enough. It can only look at objects and distinguish between a glass and a table. Thought does not have anything to measure life by—life is too vast.

In moments when the mind is silent, we can apprehend a directional dynamic. We are in that flow and label ourselves as a person in the world of named objects—a glass, a table. In fact, we don't know what we are.

We can call ourselves anything we wish, or we can try to speak through and from that flow. Our challenge is to align in the expression of that in our life, to speak and live from that flow and to allow the shift of form that comes in what is next. Transformation then is the contact of the unlimited with form.

Creativity is what is left over when we take apart what we know and what we have been told. What is next is left to express itself. How can whatever we learned yesterday with this master, that book, or that philosophy help us with what is next? It has to be invented right now.

The passage to what is next is through nonexistence. Enter the nothingness of all of the known reality, and for those who dare to die to what is known, there is a gift. That gift is what we often call fear. Fear is the resistance to nonexistence. This resistance is the creative force that presents us with reality, with existence itself. Without this, there is nonexistence.

From the perspective of mind, the unknown is its annihilation—the collapse of reality and an entry into nothingness. There is something in the universe, not nothing, and this something is the expression of an energetic movement, a resistance to the underlying emptiness. The mind sees this as a Kali-esque energy. What we call fear is our interpretation of that creative energetic movement. We experience the contraction of the holding on, the clinging, the referencing back in time. If our interpretation is abandoned, then fear is energy, and creative energy at that. It is the same non-dual energy that is flowing through all of life.

In this energy, reality is a marvelous thing. It can suggest that there is something where there is nothing. If I am talking to my mother, I am a son. If I talk to an employer, I am the worker. If I talk to my yoga teacher, I am a yogi. So what story shall I tell? There is no such thing as a seeker, there is just someone who is fearful, who wants power, who wants control, who believes that through some knowledge he can find some place in the universe.

Reality has something unreal about it—a mystery that suggests itself to us. If we look at our life, was there ever a time when reality was so concrete, so clear, that there was no mystery? From our very first breath, we all know the question: What is real? Is there something or nothing? With the first inhalation we had something, but we then had to give the breath back, and we had nothing. Then we took another breath. We sit in actuality in this interchange, and yet we are so definitely identified in the body and in such resistance to nothingness. We know we are not autonomous, we are not substantial, but if someone calls our name, we always respond.

The personality has built itself up by the biological imperative of survival. And a narrative is created through the environment, such as the suggestions of the parents: *You are such a good boy, That was right and that was wrong,* and so on. This psychobiological circumstance becomes a personality with an aggressive nature, a shy nature, and a thousand and one other attributes.

But the question *What is actual?* is there also, and that question is part of everyone's package. We are all seekers and finders at the same time; the question is in fact not a question, it is knowing that what looks to be real, really isn't so. The edifice of the personality is information that we use to express that knowledge.

Spiritual realization is a fiction, part of the mythology of the culture of seeking. Such spiritual fiction makes for good books and lecture tours, and, of course, for gathering followers or explaining to ourselves why we are indulging in the laziness of being followers. There are some who tell their story of enlightenment, but they largely have been followed by scandals or are quite occupied with messianic power trips. We can imagine a person who is constantly in that sort of state, but they would be brain damaged, on drugs, or have a brain anomaly that could hardly be useful to others.

Gurus, masters, sages, lawyers, accountants, shopkeepers, bus drivers, mothers, fathers—all these roles are "inhabited" by fine people who are doing what they think they need to do based on their identity. This is the human condition.

The risk of creation is a radical trust in transformation, a relationship to life that is not in struggle with what occurs, recognizing that life is creating and that what it creates is what is next.

NON-DUALITY

THERE IS NO MORE THAN ONE. YOU CAN THINK ABOUT MORE THAN one thing, but that remembering is also one.

An intellectual understanding of this unitive fact invites lack of responsibility, and we might like a world where everything is just happening according to some higher and distant source. It is great if there is no free will, because then we can continue to be jerks and have a great philosophical explanation for our narcissism. If we happen upon an integrated unity, not just the idea of it, then we discover ourselves as the higher source with the accountability for the whole expression of life. Life is the complete responsibility for what is next—that is the quantum world.

Time doesn't exist in the quantum world. When we think about it, talk about it, and try to use words to refer to it, there is a before and an after. We can talk about it, but is it possible to experience it directly right now? Can we touch that? Shall we create world peace right now?

The mind can't say *yes*. What actually occurs is our resistance and conditioning. We say, *this can't be*. But, if the mind doesn't say, *this can't be,* then can it be so? In the full human potential dramatic shifts are as possible as the status quo.

For world peace to happen, *I* have to stop happening. The potential world is brushing up against our reality and the mind that resists the potential of that quantum reality. This contact is what we call transformation. We only have what is next, and it is vibrant.

If you put a dual world into one world, then there is a dynamic energy. Consciousness in contact with mind is transforming. It is a fluid universe that will change from whatever form it may be to what is next after now. This occurs outside of time and process, without cause or effect. What is next emerges from nonexistence and occurs in pure being. If we conceptualize it we will place it in time and we will tend to divide it into thinking and consciousness. That is how we perceive it.

The question is then: is my life a life of transformation, fully open to this fluid universe? There is a movement to express communion with all beings. When people come together recognizing this and to find its expression, that is a transformational space. We can go deeply into that until we find resistance. That resistance is then explored, because that is what there is in actuality. This resistance is not a problem or an error, but rather the movement of the creative. Embedded in that is the release of change.

Some will say let life flow, and others will say change your life. Let us see the possibility that life will go its own way *and* we need to change it. They are not opposites. Our need to change it is life's flow. That is the transformation. The whole that touches the fragment—life moving through us, changing us as we change life, just as consciousness touches thoughts and changes them.

We embody the movement of life. This is where non-duality can get stuck: *Things go just as they go, so be it.* What happens when passion appears? Passion—not as an emotion, but as an energy that often has emotion as a by-product. An analytical approach does not address what comes next after we see life as it is, perfectly in balance, and everything just happening on its own. That is all true, *and* it is a magical and fluid universe that is energetic and transformational. We can get caught in the pristine beauty of non-duality as a philosophy. We can address everything with non-duality, but we can't live it, because living is passionate, involved, transformational. Passion is the constant confrontation of the relative world by the absolute energy of the universe.

Passion has nothing to do with experience. Experience has to do with trying to contain things in good and bad, pleasurable and unpleasurable. Passion has to do with a dynamic next, not a static, self-hypnotized, being-in-the-present now, which so many purveyors of awareness have sold us. Passion takes action, undertakes something, creates.

Non-duality takes you along the way of the "negative," and there it is untouchable. You can't reach truth by the positive way; you have to do that by deconstruction. But after you have deconstructed everything, then what? Is it nothing? Is it something? Or does expression take place? We don't live it as everything or nothing. We live something else, and that is the collision between the not-something and the something, the total with the relative, the fragment with the formless.

The mind will never know, because it only sees a fragment, and that is not relevant to the expression of the creative universe.

We tell each other that kind of story—that there is something to learn. In actuality, there is nothing to learn, so much as there is something that has to be lived. We *do* see it, just not using thought. Are we ready to live in simultaneous existence and nonexistence?

Can the human being embody form and openness; can we stay in contact with the life stream and integrate that fluidity into function? It is not so difficult to be special when you are in front of a room full of people who are projecting *he is so special*. Or you can go to an ashram and sit silently. But that's not remarkable; rather what *is* astonishing is that any of us is capable of living in the frenetic culture of the contemporary world.

Do you think Ramana Maharshi could have raised your children, worked at your job, handled your mother or father, met the challenges that cross your path every day? And if they put you in Ramana Maharshi's chair and people started worshipping you, what would happen to you?

Living is the ultimate question. It is not a question of the mind and it is not answerable, it is what is very much alive right now, and the good news is we are all immersed in it, wherever we may be and whoever we may be. There is nothing extraordinary about this ultimate question, and that is what is so interesting. No guidance, no teacher, is going to answer that question for you. Life is the ultimate question, so let us plunge into it completely.

CRACKING

THE

CONDITIONING

IT IS NOT THROUGH ANY PRACTICE THAT YOU WILL FIND YOUR WAY out of the conceptual into the actual. Relentlessly doing nothing about the conditioning, abandoning any improvement, embracing the actual in whatever form—this is the purification that is so easy to avoid with spiritual materialism.

The actual is unpleasantly insistent on the absence of any self and no credit is given for this realization. There is no reward, there is just what is, and *what is* is not something, it is what is next.

We idealize the transformative life into a life of power, of extraordinary experience, of deep realization. It is none of these things; rather it is a life that is without a trace, a life as it actually is, which is without *me*.

That transformation is to lose everything is an understatement so vast as to be without meaning. One has to lose everything, and one has to lose the one who has lost everything, and one has to lose the experience of losing everything, and one has to lose the narrative that gives meaning to losing everything, and one cannot even rest in the nihilism that is so attractive in the black hole of total loss of all perspective, meaning, and purpose. In the complete collapse into this black hole there is a mutation in unrecognizable form, an entry into a new universe into which we are expelled from the total compression we have understood as loss. Even that loss is lost in the creation of what is next.

We cannot organize an actual life around loss any more than we can organize it around acquisition. We cannot systemize an actual life in any way, and we are left as a simple function of the organizational expression of life where once we believed so fervently that we were the organizer. There is no credit for that, no fame, no recognition—this deal is so one-sided and without benefit to us that we will do anything to avoid it.

We dodge it because a marriage to the energy of life is an invitation for it to course through our life, every cell, every idea, every relationship, every social structure, and to change the fixed to the fluid and back again—and again and again. All that is not available will break down and be recreated before the life energy will sustain us.

We steer clear of this energy because we are most comfortable when we look in the mirror in the morning and have some recollection of who we see. We find profound disturbance in waking from a deep sleep into a moment where there is no sense of location, of who, what, where, when, and how. We construct busily all day long to keep the disturbance at bay, to substantiate our reality and solidity. The disturbance is the energy of life, surging through our system, knocking at the doors of our perception.

The energy of life is unconcerned about our constructions, the sense of self on which we expend so much neurotic capital. Our persona can be used by this energy or ignored. We may find ourselves expressing and functioning in ways that have nothing to do with our idea of self and we may find that we must utilize the very self that we have come to realize is only a chimera. The life energy is intelligent and fluid, and while we occupy ourselves with the care and feeding of our imagined identity, the actual flows through us and manifests as what is next.

We can continue our quest for improvement or not. We can search for happiness, enlightenment, security, or identity, or not. The search is not wrong; it is unrelated to the actual. We do not have to search for the manifest; it is what we are, and where we find actuality is not in time and not in the now, but in the discovery of what is next.

Can we accelerate this discovery, can we activate it, can we undergo transformation, can we do anything to trigger this release? We can do anything we would like, but in a universe without causation, without location, without discrimination, this doing is not doing, it is not action in actuality, but simply the bubbling of ideas empty of substance, anchored in nothing. The universe is not doing anything, nor are we. Manifestation is not an action, and it is not a thing. God is not a verb or a noun.

This is a non-conceptual inquiry that involves the entirety of our life and everything this life touches. That something else is directing life, regardless of our realization of it, is an entirely different question if in fact I am the something else. Drop time, location, and meaning and we are the direction of life. Is this another enlightenment game? In post-spirituality the idea of improvement of any kind is absurd, leaving the enlightenment game equally so.

The reality that encases is so embedded in our identity that it is usually only through tragic circumstances that it is shattered. There is something else that can shatter us with an unbearable and mysterious force. We can call it love, although that word is encumbered, but nevertheless it has to do with a transformational shift in the perspective, or a loss of the identity with the reality that encloses us.

This movement, whether you call it love or tragedy, comes about through the collision of our reality with the actual. It is dying from the perspective of the structure built around the *me* and from our subjective experience we experience it as a traumatic shift. The map of reality no longer applies, and it ceases in an abrupt way, where time doesn't function. From the perspective of totality that shift doesn't exist, because the relative structure never existed.

NO MORALITY

Essentially it's a shift that gets people to see a difference between moralistic judgments and need-serving judgments, or life-serving judgments. Moralistic judgments are those built on an old fashioned theology that implies that human beings are very lazy and evil and violent. Therefore the corrective process is penitence. You have to make them hate themselves for what they've done, to believe that they deserve to suffer for what they've done. The paradigm shift is away from that to a shift of judging in terms of whether things serve life or not. And if they don't, to create the quality of connection between people that helps people to enjoy contributing to one another's well being.

—Marshal Rosenberg

POST-SPIRITUALITY IS THE TOTAL ABSENCE OF MORALITY. MORALITY is, after all, a construction based on belief systems, religious considerations, or abstract philosophical treatises. There is the deep cultural belief that morality is reflective of an underlying reality, but the actual universe appears to be amoral. It is not immoral but rather has no orientation at all to morality. This is a shattering realization in that there is no basis for understanding good or evil, or for determining the action that is good or evil.

We have developed elaborate descriptions of the moral life, as if this conceptualization somehow determines what occurs. For those who remain within the moral construct, there is only dismay at those who step beyond. For those who step beyond, there is redemption only in accepting the moral majority and denouncing the transgression. A careful examination of all moral systems shows only confusion in the guise of truth, yet few will admit that confusion is the truth.

Moral systems break down in the face of life because elaborate as they are, they cannot encompass the chaotic generation of reality that life produces. It is not a universe that runs like a clock—mechanical, predictable, and knowable. Rather it is a universe that is expressed as the ultimate creative act of acausality, without regard for the conceptual constructs of me, you, and us. Meanwhile, the me, you, and us are busy conceptualizing the actions we believe that we are making that are good or evil, as if we sat back somewhere at a control panel choosing to pull the lever marked *good* because we are good, or the lever marked *bad* because we are bad.

Theologians suggest this is a soul-directed life, because without this center there is no meaning in religion. If there is no doer, then there can be no sin, no redemption. An acausal universe has no place for religion, and religion has no function, as it can neither describe the universe nor control it. A wrathful God can be appeased, a loving God can be adored, but an acausal God can only deliver chaos and confusion, cosmic creativity, and random destruction. No religion could contain acausality, non-location, and timelessness, yet this appears to be the actual nature of the universe.

Our religion, in whatever form we have come to believe, is a denial of the actual. In this, religion functions very well, not in containing the truth of the universe, but in partitioning it from our realization. We hardly have the capacity to absorb the reality of life, and we are easily satisfied with the mythic stories that religion hands us.

The price we pay for our religion is the immense weight of morality, a code of behavior that is both untrue and impossible to live. First, we have to have control over our actions, which we do not have. And secondly, we have to want to live a moral life, which we certainly do not want to do.

What we do have is a desire system that contravenes the moral system, and we have no absolute control over our actions in any event. This is a setup for failure, and moral failure is the lifeblood of religion. Religion thrives on the paternal qualities of punishment and the maternal quality of redemption. Morally, we are destined to fail, then be punished and redeemed.

When we are moral, it is constructed to please ourselves. When we are immoral, we are either hidden or exposed, and it is in exposure that we must ritualize our recovery as a moral being. The strategies embedded in our moral structures have to do with maintaining power and control. When what we want is within the moral code, then we hold power, and when it is not, we must operate in the shadow and pay the price of penance or, worse—crucifixion—for what is forbidden. We confess, we have failed, we are wrong, we are bad, but never do we admit that we have actually gotten what we wanted, and the mea culpa is only access to more of the same. We are not moral and immoral people; we are amoral and strategic— the strategy retrofitted to the action already enacted.

Dare we throw out the whole game and admit to our amoral state and our actions that have no obvious actor attached? There is no redemption, because there is no sinner.

The problem, of course, is that while I might be pleased with the notion of living an amoral life, free from the retribution of guilt, it also means that you are doing so as well. This poses a problem of a different dimension, because I can no longer be sure that I will get the best of this chaotic new world. Better that we agree to a code of conduct and hide the transgressions. It is a reasonable approach, and the only quandary is that it is untrue. Regardless of our moral code, the expression of that morality is only circumstantial; it is not under my control, nor is it under yours.

On the quantum level the occurrence of reality is chaotic and acausal. On the macro-physical level our cognition of our actions happens a split second after the actual occurrence, in that our cognition is reflective, not generative. On a behavioral level we are a collection of genes and memes, biological imperatives, and conditioned concepts. On a social level we act in concert or reaction, but without possibility of autonomy. On a cosmic level we know absolutely nothing useful in our conceptual framework. Where is the controller, the moral agent, the doer?

It is a kind of madness to enter into an acausal, amoral world in which no punishment or reward moderates the actual arising of our manifest behavior. It is a deeper insanity to realize that we cannot even know what this behavior is once it has occurred. Yet this is the madness in which we live every day. It is just that we live in denial of it by constructing the idea of a mechanical and predictable universe in which autonomous individuals move and act in right or wrong ways, depending on whether they are good or evil. This story is satisfying, but it is agitated by the abrupt occurrences of conditions and phenomena that do not fit. We are appeased by the notion that science will explain this with time, theologians will wrestle with the explanation of evil, the social structures will enact programs and laws to attend to whatever emerges. The emperor has no clothes; morality does not have existence in an acausal universe, other than as a constructed agreement that lets us each sleep at night. Or not.

If we cannot see the actual for the moral story then we are left to struggle for a moral world that makes sense, even though it does not, and it cannot. For many this engagement with the impossible will occupy a life.

If we see clearly that there is no point in moralism in the face of acausality, then we have a very different challenge and one that is no less daunting than the abandonment of morality. That question is, what is it that expresses out of an amoral life, in fact, and can we live in that actuality. Can we trade morality for actualism? There is the cultural idea that destruction and evil will be the result. But in amorality there is no more pull to immorality than there is to morality.

In acausality, there is no result, there is only the expression of the quantum potential in the energetic movement, occurring not in the moment, but exploding out of the moment into what is next. Why would that be evil? Why would it be destructive? We cannot say with any certainty what it will be, until it is. And then, we cannot describe it with any clarity, because it is not. We have entered a reality of possibility, of what is next, but it is entirely energetic or non-material. To give it materiality we have to fix it, damp down the potential, hold it to form, give it location and time. This means describing it, and that description will be of the past, from which all descriptions are generated. Whether this is the multi-millisecond delay in the cognitive description of a bodily occurrence that is so fast that it appears to be the cause of the action, or whether it is the psychological construction of a memory that suggests that something concrete happened to an experiencer, all experience is of the past and has no actual utility in our understanding of the dynamic potential of what is next.

What is next is amoral, and that fact tells us nothing about it, because the quantum potential expressed has nothing to do with good or evil. If we place ourselves in that expression without the safety line of the past, without the ballast of experience, we step beyond good and evil into the unknown. Whatever is manifest will remain forever unknown, even as it passes from unmanifest to manifest to experience, because experience is always an interpretive lie, and the truth of manifestation exists only in its occurrence, not in its reflection.

To live in what's next is to live in continuous unknowing. The structure of mind is hardly useful to navigate the unknown, much as it would be pointless to drive a car down a highway by gazing only in the rearview mirror. Perhaps it is better to drive without looking at all than to look back, because back doesn't predict what is next. Without looking, there is at least the introduction to all other sensing, to what is beyond sensing, to everything else. In the unknown, without depending on thought, there is everything else. The exploration of the conceptual, which we may have called religion, philosophy, or spirituality, expands to include that everything. Everything defies the notion of a category, so we cannot call it something, we can only call it not-something, or post-something. We can only use the sense of everything to constantly abandon the limitations of what we have come to know.

There is no good and evil in a non-dual world. The universe is just what it is. There is creation and destruction in the universe. But destruction isn't evil. Destruction is what precedes creation. We do not want to experience what we call "negative energies" like fear, violence, or anger. We only want to experience the "good" energies. Mind sorts experiences into the ones it wants and likes and the ones it doesn't like, and tries to create a world in which it only has what it likes and doesn't have what it doesn't like. This is a completely hopeless task in an aqualitative universe, but this is what mind does. Unpleasant energies are important. When you walk in front of a car, fear is important.

If you live in an Islamic culture, your idea of what is good and evil is different from what it would be if you lived in a Christian context. We fight each other, kill each other, commit relative good and evil over these ideas. Does the universe really have these ideas as some kind of archetype? Look at it from the broadest view possible: the creation of matter and the destruction of matter. Is it a good act or is it an evil act? The universe is unconcerned.

If I can convince you that there is good and evil, and particularly that you are evil and I am good, or that I know what is good and evil and you don't—then there is a lot of power in that. The creation of good and evil is power. We attempt to control the universe by dividing it into good and evil, by judging it.

How do we function and express without having this distinction? It is not through distinctions, but rather through the collapse of those distinctions, that something new can emerge. Our lives are very complicated; when we start to apply rather simple notions of good and bad to a complicated life, we find that we are just confused. If we think of confusion as bad, then we have to get rid of it. We have to go to some authority who is going to help us with that and who tells us what is good and what is evil. But could we just simply face the fact that we are confused?

Confusion is really no place to stand. Con-fusion is really the fusion from form to form. This is the perception of what is actual. The fusion of form to form is energy, and if the world is energetic, then we don't have the ability to divide it. It is an undivided universe, and, in that, good and evil are not essentially different. The energy of life is beyond good or evil; it is a continuum. If we embrace life as unitive energy, there is no energy to avoid. If we believe that we exist in a location, then that sense of location and the divisions that come from that create all kinds of ideas—some good and some evil. When the sense of location breaks down, then where will we stand to start dividing up the world? What we are left with in a non-located reality is an energetic world. Tell me about good and evil in terms of an energetic world, a world in which there is no time, no location, no meaning, no existence. Where is good and evil?

Once you locate yourself, then, for instance, anything that is attacking is evil. Anything that opposes you is evil. If there is no identity, no location, then what is an attack?

We can see the chance for change in our own lives in connection with our children, our relationships, our work, and our spiritual journey. The "negative" spaces that we call tragedy, violence, or fear are openings for a shift to take place. Rather than step into what is next, we run from it. We run toward the solace of our belief systems when we have a possibility of the breakdown of what we know, including the fracturing of our spiritual ideals.

With the assumption of good and bad, we have to run from the fracturing toward the unity. In actuality we run from an idea of separation to an idea of unity and call this the spiritual path. This is going deeper into illusion. For example, what should we do with the separation we experience with our anger? We don't know anything about our anger. We are too busy reacting to it, suppressing it, modifying it, expressing it, dividing it into pieces, until we are left in contact only with our concept of what anger is. Anger as an energy is the same as love as an energy. It is one energy.

We can try to cultivate good energies like compassion. It is relatively better to be doing less harm than more harm. But if we are creating time—the idea of progression through spiritual practice—then aren't we also creating the opposite of that? What about everything else that is moving through time? If you look at the world as it is and run it out through time, you don't find that compassion is going to predominate. A compassionate world isn't going to be created. Is there anything else at play besides progress through time—the development of compassion through practice, like some frequent flyer program where if you spend enough hours on your cushion you get the reward of a compassionate world?

This goes to the question of the directionality of life, and this is not about time. Totality, moving through thought, has directionality to it. It doesn't include time, because totality is not in time. Time is within thought. Once we're in thought, in that relative world, it is better to be ethical than unethical. It is better to be nice than not nice. But stepping outside of that reality, something else is there. Totality is transforming reality, and the directionality of that movement is not in time and not related to our goodness.

We suggest to ourselves that we should be different from what we are. We try to alter ourselves when instead we could be asking, *What is it that's happening?* In this inquiry we can begin to look at the drives, the habits, the needs that are being expressed.

If you try to be different, you step into a process in time, into improvement, into separation. In separation you see the world out there, and changing that objectified world becomes the source of your happiness or discontent. That is violence.

We cannot fully engage the question of violence with the assumptions that we carry around, we can only engage in our assumptions. And from those assumptions flows a world of good and evil.

If we leave the world of good and evil, then we are in energy and in the risk of creativity. We can assign *destructive, creative, sustaining* to that, but we cannot really see where one aspect begins and the other ends.

Let us not have the illusion that we are freer than the world. We are the world. We don't stand outside of it. There is no place of stillness that is not also movement.

Whether we are in a monastery or on a battlefield, wherever we find ourselves, could we ask the question *What is this?*—not as an intellectual question, but as the absorption and integration of the energy of that place.

The energy of life is beyond good and evil. The flow of energy is the movement out of this moment. What's next doesn't give a damn about our good and evil—thankfully.

THE ILLUSION OF SELFLESSNESS

A PERSON OF SPIRITUAL VALUES IS ONE WHO ASPIRES TO ACT SELF-lessly. But such an aspiration is a dream within a dream, the ideal of a *me* to act like *no me*. Selfless action is the illusion of self suggesting to itself a transcendent expression of the illusion.

Facing the unrelenting nature of an acausal universe, the ideal of selfless action is shattered.

The drive to selflessness is an expression of a deep neurosis—a construction of despair, depression, and lack that seeks a positive projection. A selfless person would do better to look to the source of their fear and insecurity than to attempt to emulate the tired adages of religious sensibilities that admonish us to act without regard for ourselves. This unfortunate construct leaves us acting selfishly and demeaning ourselves at the same time for not being better. We are selfish, not selfless. The idea of selflessness is an avoidance of what is actual.

We may be biologically designed to act with aggression or submission, to protect our family or group, to sacrifice for our offspring, even to have brain receptors structured for empathy. None of our natural makeup appears to support selflessness as a generalized way of being.

There is a fundamental difference between recognizing the need and the potential for the transmutation of selfishness in the human condition and the attempt to evoke the ideal of selflessness through spiritual or psychological technology. Selfishness no longer works well in the contemporary world, yet this is what we are. We cannot replace what we are with what we wish we could be, we can only create the pretense of change in this fashion. Actual change occurs without our control or planning and despite our ideas of goodness.

CHANGE

THE PREDICTIVE MIND SUGGESTS TO US THAT THERE IS A KNOW-able future. Acausality suggests that there is not. Worse, without the utility of predictability, we are left with change—not just rapid change, but continuous, unrelenting change.

Thought builds its resistance in an attempt to keep out this onslaught, but despite the complexity of our defenses, change attends our life. Our thought structures, our relationships, our social organizations, and our business systems are in denial of this. They are not fluid enough to embrace the energetic reality of continuous change. In total, they are a resistance to the actual movement, and, at the same time, allow the buildup of potential before the surge of manifestation.

The image is of a dam, which blocks the flow of a river, but in so doing stores the energy of the movement. Upon the release of water, tremendous force is unleashed that can destroy or generate. As the dam is built continuously higher, the water builds behind it. The engineering becomes increasingly difficult, the pent-up potential becomes increasingly destructive, and there is diminishing possibility of creativity without collapse. Eventually, our metaphoric dam will collapse, the pressure of the water will overwhelm it, and the force of the water will change what is before it.

Is it necessary to build the resistance to change ever higher or is there an optimum height and an intelligent release of the force? Can we ride this change, rather than resist it? Is there an accelerator of change that allows the creative force by accepting the destructive aspect?

In our lives and in our organizations, we are faced with these questions as the force of change travels through our constructed systems. Change is what is actual, and any intelligent organization will embody rapidly shifting conditions as its essence.

PART 4

LOVE
AND THE
TRANSACTUAL
REALITY

Instead of being so bound up with everyone,
be everyone.

When you become that many, you're nothing.

Empty.

—Rumi

WHAT IS LOVE?

N OW THAT WE ARE NOT HERE, WE CAN USE THE WORD *LOVE*. BUT what is love? We can see what love is not. Love is not the romance that we've been trained to experience. It's not the idea that comes from movies and books. It's not the acquisition of something from another—the expectation that the other is going to fill my emptiness. It has nothing at all to do with feeling good, with romance, or with getting something.

The nature of the lover is this grasping, clawing, grabbing quality in us that wants to possess something to give us a sense of our own location. Love is beyond the lover, beyond the *me*. Love is that which actually connects. It doesn't want anything, because it already has everything. The lover experiences the desire for love as this kind of longing, because he cannot get to that place of connection.

We have no means to get to love. We can't come close to it, we can't get far from it. The structure of the lover is not even in the same universe. That is why it is so frustrating and difficult, why relationship is the most confusing part of our lives. We construct love within this idea of self to self, me to you, subject to object. It is always divided.

Relationships are usually a disaster because the construction isn't stable. You and I construct an agreement with each other in order to have a loving relationship. That agreement is based on a kind of image. We meet each other in some restaurant, you have a nice smile. The agreement is that you will always have a nice smile, because that is what has attracted me to you. And my agreement may be that I am going to say kind words to you. But the reality is that a day or a week or a month later your smile goes, my kind words go, and we have something else. And now we've broken the agreement, we feel abandoned and hurt. Then we seek to fix that. We go to a therapist or a counsellor. From now on you try to smile and I will try to say kind words, and if we don't, we immediately apologize and try harder. We have a new agreement that patches up the old agreement. Soon we have these historic agreements that are just endless. We need a law book in order to talk to each other since we can't keep track of the agreements anymore. Of course, your law book is written in the language of your reality, your memory, your constructed history, and my law book is written in my subjective reality.

Our own history, our agreements, and our fixes of the agreements weigh down our relationships. The whole negotiation that we construct around love has nothing to do with love. Love is absolutely still. There is no sense of "self" in it.

It is striking when we touch love in the transactual reality, where the actual moves undivided. We step out of our construction for one moment and touch the actuality of energy and silence as one. Time stops. It is a glimpse of the possible universe of connectedness. If we could let that be, if we could just be still in that, then that quality of connectedness might be ongoing.

When you experience that expansive feeling at the beginning of a relationship, you have the implicit promise that you will always be able to go back to that. The idea of love being about a particular feeling quality is the problem. You will never be able to go back to it. That's the beauty of transactual love. It moves from actual to actual, without time or location. It's like a shooting star. You can't go back. It is just gone as it happens. A flower is going to drop its petals and will never have that same blossom again. It may have a different blossom, but never the same. Transactual love is an ephemeral quality that is never the same, it occurs outside of the individuated reality that we are used to operating from, without past or future, without meaning.

If you see the relationship to another as encompassing all possibilities, then you can never be disappointed and it can move in freedom. This is so much more spectacular than anything that we could build out of our memory of what the movies and the books tell us romance is. If you stand still, then you are always in stillness.

We can fall crushingly in love throughout each day with everyone we meet, because there is a constant in life that is occurring. It's an evanescent energetic state in which we do not have to do anything in particular. There is no requirement of *me*. I don't have to express it or suppress it. It's just a simple, beautiful movement of energy in stillness. When we are at a loss for words, that must be the silence speaking.

The search for the lover outside who is going to complete me is a projection of this *me*. A concept can only see its own concepts. It can only see what it already knows. This searcher for love is searching for self-as-whole, but it doesn't work.

We can search to be the perfect lover. But that too is futile. We are constructed to be terrible lovers, always manipulating the other to get what we want. There is no way out of this strategic approach that makes up our mind. There is no way to reform it; there is no way to be better. Give up the whole notion that there is anything to do about that and be finished with the idea of being a perfect lover or finding a perfect lover.

The beloved is already in your life, right now. It's the person you are looking at right now. It's the person you are going to see on the street. It's the person you will see when you walk through the door of your home. The beloved is you, and what you see is what you are. It's the depth of your own heart.

In the conceptual mind it can only be about getting something, grabbing something, grasping something. When you step outside the conceptual mind, then you are automatically in your own heart and in love with everything. There is no preparation; it's what is next.

Do you really want that? This is a fundamental question. We can talk all the spiritual language about love, but we may in fact just want to go to the next bar and pick up a new partner and start all over again. Let us not fool ourselves that we have gone beyond.

We are not beyond the biological imperative for reproduction that is primary to the organism. The genetic pattern, which is *me*, demands the reproduction of *me* biologically. This is one of the most basic urges—to come together with another person, to reproduce, which today translates into having sexual relations whether reproduction is possible or not.

Anything that resists what is actual is going to be suffering. If you go to a religious organization that doesn't believe in sexual expression, then they will say *you shouldn't*. If you go to a religious organization that says that free love is good, then they will say *you should*.

But who is suffering all the anxiety of the *shoulds* and *shouldn'ts?* What is generating personality? Go to the core of the question and you will come to the identification with the

sense of *me,* the fear of death, and the resistance to that annihilation in the creation of this mentalized world.

Unfortunately the conceptual *me* is unstable. It comes
and it goes each moment. The experience of that changing
center is the recognition that *I* am not substantial, that I am
dying in each moment. And there is the fear that the conditioned *me* won't arise again.

How do I conquer death? The conceptual mind can't stop
the *me* from dying in each moment. It can't stop the body
from dying at the end of my life. And it knows that. So it creates a mythic world, in which it can stop death by finding a
younger woman, taking the woman of another man, finding a
powerful man, or destroying a powerful man—showing that I
am still young, that I am more powerful, that I can defeat
death.

The true usefulness of relationship is that the conditioning
comes into the relationship, and we then see it as pain, as dif-
ficulty, as conflict, as contraction. That is how we know that
there is something that we need to look into. The value of relationship is that it's going to dig up all of our stuff and put it right
back in our face. There is value in standing absolutely still in
relation to the other, just as they are, with all the irritations,
and all the things that really hurt. Then every relationship is
perfect.

Don't say, "The problem is you!" to the other, but see that
the whole of the relationship is a representation of mind. We
wanted deep meditation and amazing spiritual experiences,
and we got it! This kind of messiness instructs us to totally
abandon any ideas of relationship and allow a kind of simple
intelligence to arise. We are not above or beyond the kind of
issues that arise in relationship. We could use the metaphor
that we are "riding the tiger" in relationship. Sometimes the

tiger turns around and bites you. Even so, you can never get off without being devoured.

We can know all of this, but there is a difference between realization and integration. There is a difference between the experience of interconnectedness—the enlightenment that is not there—and staying with the creative flow of that connection as we ride the tiger into what is next.

Transactual love is really quite simple. It's available in each moment to anyone. But that realization of stillness has to live as a hyperfluid dynamic. This is where it is a challenge to give up the safety of the spiritual now and step into what is next.

Bring the realization into the body, the relationships, the work, and see what happens as we slam up against the infrastructure of mind. The mind is very, very resistant. That is where spirituality dies. Transactual love is not alive in the spiritual theories of spiritual teachers in spiritual settings with spiritual acolytes. In these temples of delusion, spirituality is sacrificed to the gods of relative reality.

Where spirituality is least likely is where it is most vital—in the actual life and circumstances of the common person. It's very easy to be a spiritually special person when you are protected and cared for like a child, always in comfortable and nice environments. You can take most anybody and put them on a cushion in a nice room with a lot of admiration and they would be likely to express great enlightenment. But put them in a house with a gaggle of kids, bills to pay, and a job to go to, and let us see how the enlightenment goes.

Those of us who are very interested in the integration of realization will have to face life—all of life. That is what love demands.

What is love? It is not a thing but an energetic connection without opposite. It has nothing to do with getting anything.

Loving is the radical abandonment of my construction, my ideas—the total acceptance of life just as it is, unknowing, undivided. Love occurs, as it becomes what is next, and just before we declare it is now.

AUTONOMY
AND
MERGER

T HE SWEEPING ENERGY OF LOVE DESTROYS ALL SENSE OF SEPA-ration. With this immense shift in perspective comes the challenge of finding boundaries within which to function in our day-to-day life. Love that is impersonal is not the challenge. This love is easy, because it wants nothing, needs nothing, and gives its own spaciousness to every relationship that occurs in the relative world. But can this impersonal love enter into that relative world? Can it touch and transform the personal, the attached, the romantic relationship, or must it always stay outside—an observer of the sticky love that most of us find so confusing? Here resides the question of autonomy and merger—the relative love of me/you and the absolute love of non-separation. This question is not an intellectual question, it is not an emotional question, nor is it even an energetic question, but rather a transformative question, one that is asked and answered in the full living of the movement into the relative world.

We have come to think of our spirituality as a detachment from the world or, perhaps for those who are more sophisticated, we may consider a post-detachment existence of returning to a regular life. But this detachment, whether disconnected from the illusion of life or re-entering the day-to-day life as a kind of demonstration of its non-substantiality, misses the point entirely. The post-spiritual reality suggests something entirely more challenging, which is to live life fully, including the personal attachments, the wild emotions, the neurotic thoughts, and the painful body experiences. This living is without recourse to an observer, or to any detachment, any space around the experience. It is the complete surrender to life as it is, without any consideration of changing it, distancing from it, controlling it.

We found ourselves in a life that was characterized by fear and expressed as spirituality. We were overwhelmed by our anxiety, our drives, our failures, our loneliness, and sought the solace of the spiritual practice, the fellow travelers, the teachers of tranquility or transmitters of energy states. But really, we were afraid of living naked and raw, wrecked by our own imbalance and the drives that haunted us. We feared this consuming energy and looked for ways to harness it or at least to ride it through our life to the things we craved.

The psychotherapeutic world, the spiritual world, the religious world—all promised a respite, gave us hope, and offered ritual and activity to distract us from the surging force of our own contact with the life stream. In the end these forms and practices simply failed; they too were subsumed into the churning waters of our fear. Far from the answer to our anxiety, these solutions simply amplified our panic. We never really had faith in these forms, we had only a kind of weak and false hope that they would bring us faith, delivered packaged and easy, requiring nothing from us but to show up and pay the fees. The therapies, the spirituality and religions, gave us their failure, a perfect reflection of what we brought to these forms.

Left exhausted by our efforts to hide from our life, we try to manage our experience with the technology of our psycho-spiritual practices. We try awareness but find only a disconnected observer. We try surrender but find only resistance to what we don't like. We try renunciation but find only attractions and obsessions. We try non-dualism but discover that we are enmeshed in structures of mind that are always living in separation. We try tantra and find that living in the expression of our drives is just as empty as living in detachment from them.

Every attempt to characterize and control our life leaves us failed and flattened. Yet life keeps pouring through our system, unrelenting, unconcerned, uncaring about all our efforts to understand, to change, to surrender. Life just does not care about our ideas, our emotions, our structures, that attempt to assign time, location, and meaning. Life crashes into us with abandon, incinerates our precious moment, and moves us without hesitation into what is next.

This fundamental energy—the movement of life—is what it is, with or without our understanding or interpretation. It doesn't even require that we understand that. The energy of life is expressing itself as what we are, unrelated to our imaginings that it is *we* who are accessing the energy to become something better. In this, all of our efforts to get to that energy are pointless, since the simple fact is that we are the manifestation of that energy, just as we are.

This energy takes us directly to where we do not want to go—to the life we have run from, the life that is so confusing and fragmented. It takes us to our life as it is, stripped of the veneer of specialness. It takes us to the ordinary, the mundane, the attached, the personal.

Living stripped of pretense, in the full flow of life energy, we are no longer separated from the desires that make up the person that we are. The flow of wanting suggests an incoherent but nevertheless discrete aspect of life, an expression of the energy, but also easily identifiable as *me*. This *me* is the very expression of the life energy and it is the epitome of separation. This is autonomy. It is the expression of the relative state of separation as an inseparable part of the whole energy. Autonomy is driven to express from the forces that come into play in its desires and fears. It is creative in its division. What it creates is more separation and, at the same time, a deep desire for merger. It creates a life that reflects its needs but that suggests the availability to love.

Love arrives and the autonomy is swept away. Merger is so compelling that what is differentiated is submerged. But not for long.

THE
DENIAL
OF
LOVE

T HE ENERGY OF LOVE MOVES THROUGH EACH OF OUR LIVES. THIS is not a romantic quality, nor is it the spiritual ideal. Rather, it is an energy that touches us deeply and connects us fundamentally to those we meet. It is an energy that we cannot fully understand or integrate from the structures of mind and emotion we inhabit. The evidence of the power of this energy is that it can literally shatter the structures of our life at any moment. It is this shattering that the structures of our mind and emotions seek to avoid.

While the energy of love moves through all form and has no dependence on any condition whatsoever, we experience it most commonly in the reflection of our emotional world and the interpretation of those feelings in our mind. The experience of love is not love, but only a faint echo of it.

When we are swept away by another, we also realize that a force is acting on our life that we do not control and cannot understand, yet it is palpable. This is an amazing moment— the contact with energy without any interpretation and without our ability to manage it. This is not very comfortable, so we begin the management plan with the emotions leading the way, personalizing this energy, and then the mind, analyzing until we have conceptualized the energy into something known.

If we are single, then we can calculate the pathway to relationship. If we are married, we can scheme an affair or design the suppression of the feeling. If we are afraid of relationship, we can run. If we want relationship, we can go toward it.

This is the management plan, and often it appears to work. We do find or avoid relationship. But there are moments in life where this energy moves and it cannot be managed; it cannot be fit into any form we can imagine. We cannot suppress it and we cannot move in it. This energy is stirring not just to create, but also to destroy. It is moving to open up the structures of our life and perhaps to create entirely new forms.

We are touched by another, and we are married. We are touched by another, and our family, friends, or colleagues cannot fathom or accept what is occurring. We are touched by another, and the very form of our lives must be confronted and everything we hold dear is suddenly at stake. Seeing the complete risk that this energy brings into our lives, we deny that we feel this love. We go for security and safety and step back from the deep feeling that is shaking our world. We rationalize, we moralize, we ritualize, we seek help in the resistance or demand punishment if we fail in our resistance. We deny love. We become Judas.

Judas denied love, going for safety in the face of the certain destruction he faced in standing in his relationship to Jesus. The irony is that the real destruction that Judas had to bear was in this denial, in seeing what he had become in his fear. He would live, but without life, with the certain knowledge that the most profound love had been thrown away.

We are all Judas in our denial of love in the small moments of each day—in our interactions with each other, the petty intrigues and conflicts and the absence of small affections. And in a more fundamental way, we all deny love when it arrives in an intense and overwhelming form. We do not stand in that energy and state its truth for all to hear. We deny it to protect our marriage, our family structures, our job, our status.

We do not say to the other, "I feel a deep energy moving in relationship to you and I have no idea what this means, but let us find out." We do not say this because it is embarrassing, humiliating, confusing, scandalous. We do not say this because we lose control. We do not state it because we can only understand it in the distortions of our mind and emotions. We can imagine the movement of this energy only in the projections of our imagination. We do not trust the intelligence of this energy to manifest and integrate in our lives, to take our lives fully to the expression of the fact of love.

Yet, if we deny this energy, our life becomes devoid of it, dried out and disconnected. The structures we live in are protected, but what is alive is waiting outside. If we open the door to this energy, we are opening the door to transformation. The forms of our life, our mind, emotions, body, family, social structure, and job do not want transformation because these structures are what will be shattered and reconstructed. These structures—what we are—will always move to deny love.

The denial of love is easily accomplished. We simply conceptualize this energy and compartmentalize it into psychological guilt, emotional manipulation, sexual power, spiritual mumbo jumbo, or religious morality. We manage this energy with our cleverness, suggesting to this one that we love and to that one that we do not. Through the description of outer word and inner fantasy we both live in this energy and refuse it in our concepts. But we never let it move in actuality. We never unify the world into a universal statement of love. We will never bring the affair home to the marriage. We will never sit still in the face of the urges that arise to sexualize the energy, or turn it to fear, or convert it to anything but what it is.

We are designed on all levels of our being to deny love. The best we can accomplish is the religious ideal, the grand concept of loving each other as ourselves. We pay homage to this ideal, but when the energy that it represents comes to call, we say it will have to wait until church on Sunday.

It is impossible for us to do anything but to deny love. And still the relentless energy of love moves to shatter us. When it does smash us, we cannot deny this energy, because all the structures designed so intricately to hold back this tidal wave have been destroyed. We are washed away. If it is not love to which our life is dedicated, then to what?

We feel compelled to do something with the movement of love. This doing tends to construct around the energy and subtly suggests that it is the construction that is love, rather than the form being the byproduct of the energy. Once we have crossed that illusionary bridge, we identify with the form (the person), and fear comes in the form of excitement (will she, won't he), and idealism (so intelligent, so beautiful, so pure). Enjoy this illusion, because it won't last, and the payment will be in pain later. The excitement wears off and becomes tedium, the idealism is crushed. This is just the actuality of form. Form changes.

The personal plays out, obscuring the essential energy. The personal will be messy, and messy will make it feel less than ideal. Less than ideal will make it seem less than love, and so forth.

We face love in the most awkward of situations, and it is often in conflict with the established relationships of our life. We may try to compartmentalize, to limit the expression, or to change partners. But there is also the possibility of making the whole movement transparent, facing it as energy and not personality, and appreciating it as such. If this love is real, then it will connect to every part of our current relationship system and not be in competition with it. Why not bring the new love that we encounter directly into our existing life and introduce it to all those who now share our life? That will be an interesting journey for all concerned and the acid test of its actuality.

The movement of love is the movement of transformation and fair warning to anyone who enters that space that we will lose everything, even what we don't know we have to lose. Love comes to destroy us and to create something entirely new from the ashes. Love is the expression of any who dare to meet in that energy, a whole heart forged from a shattered heart. Love includes all the heart, the beloved, the romantic, the broken, the devastated, and the quantum potential of what is next.

RELATIONSHIP
ON DEMAND

I N OUR INSTANT SOCIETY WITH CABLE NEWS AND ENTERTAINMENT ON demand, fast food in minutes, instant messaging in seconds, and anytime cell phones, we have attempted to consign our intimate relationships to the category of needs met on demand.

We enter into our intimacies with the desire to be fulfilled and the expectation that this will take place as a result of our relationship. In turn, we commit to that relationship and promise to do our best to meet our partner's needs. We begin to fulfill and be fulfilled, but as though we were bailing a leaky boat with a leaky bucket, we begin sinking fast in the ever-increasing complexity of our arrangement.

The pressure increases to satisfy the other, just as the unfulfilled needs in our self continue to pile up. We run, but we can't catch up. Or we stop trying, and we can no longer find our partner in the hurt, confusion, and distance that ensues.

What began as an implicit promise to fulfill each other becomes broken promises and a growing sense of neglect. We discover commitment as a smothering sense of loss of freedom rather than the ideal that we once believed in. We may even have the unpleasant insight that our intention and commitment are ineffective, in actuality contrivances, social constructions we accepted from our culture and conditioning. We may find ourselves dead in our relationship, a ghost wandering through the days of our lives, speaking but not being heard, touching but not being felt.

There is another possibility, challenging to the premise under which we encounter each other, but a possibility that relieves the pressure and complexity of partnership. This possibility challenges the very idea of partnership as an ideal. Consider the potential of a relationship that is not needs-based and not built around coercing a response to desires from each other.

We have quickly evolved our notion of relationship from one structured by power and dominance, where sex and money have been predominant forces. In the new notion of egalitarian relationship, power is shared and needs are mutually met. While this is a striking shift in perspective, it is rarely the fact in what is actual. Mutually meeting needs becomes a prolonged negotiation, resulting in compromise and a relationship more pragmatic than creative. The breakfast may get made, the kids put to bed, and everything in between accomplished each day through this political process we have come to accept as relationship, but what is lost is the passionate and risky edge that accompanied the relationship in the beginning.

We train each other to give up, to accept stability and continuity in place of fulfillment and expression. Perhaps this is what is wanted in the end. Or have we accepted this form because we cannot see any other way, because we have been conditioned by the forms around us to see only this?

If we enter into relationship with each other as an expression of passion, connection, and possibility, then isn't our interest in these qualities, not in particular to the person who appears to cause those qualities to arise? What if we stay with our attention to these qualities, not mixing them up with the form of the other person, not demanding that the other person produce these qualities in us, not blaming the other person when we can no longer find those qualities? And what if the other person does the same?

We might then have a relationship that is not on-demand: we cannot expect a response from the other; we cannot be assured that our needs are met by the other. The other person, in the same way, has no demand on us. Certainly this takes out the pressure of demand in relationship, but it also leaves open the question of fulfillment of needs.

If the relationship is built on mutual need fulfillment, then the cessation of fulfillment generally suggests an end to the form of relationship and perhaps the search for a new partner who will do better at servicing our needs and be less burdensome in their desires. But we often say to ourselves that there is not just a mutual contract but a transcendent quality we call love in our intimate partnerships, and if this is the case, then we have a challenge of a different dimension: accept love and stop trying to relate.

Having given up on the demand and the fulfillment of needs, yet finding ourselves still engaged in something we have called love, we may need to ask what the nature of our partnership is in actuality. We do not have the comfort of our former contract and we do not have the escape of denying love. We are stuck with each other and with fulfillment occurring only as it does, not as we desire. We are fulfilled when the movement in the relationship is authentically mutual, not simply because we are strident in our requirements or skillful in our negotiations.

This is a wonderfully enlightened relationship. As softer men and stronger women, we are deeply aware of our desires.

With great spaciousness we see the surging energy of these wants and the pressure for these to manifest. We accept that our partnership does not necessarily reflect these desires. We are compassionate with ourselves and with our partner. So what if we are emotionally shut down and unfulfilled, thankfully, we are enlightened, so we don't care how unhappy we are. Where we were once burdened by the maintenance of our relationship, we now live in a restful state, although psychically paralyzed from the neck down. Yoga workshops help a lot.

Is it possible that relationship can mean no demand on the other *and* the fulfillment of our needs? Can we break out of contractual relationship *and* stiflingly enlightened relationship and enter into actual relationship? Love doesn't suggest ownership or control, so why do we craft partnerships out of love that limit the creativity and expression of our self or the other? Or is what we have called love actually fear, and what we have called relationship, in fact, the attempt to control life?

Here is the possibility of something entirely different in our approach to relationship. We realize that we are together because there is a shared field we touched that we have called love. Our devotion is to this field, which happens to be manifesting the forms we see when we look at each other—and all that flows out of those forms. This field will continue to generate the forms that we will call our life. The continuity of our relationship is not ensured by our commitment, our intention, or our needs, but rather by this energetic field. Anything that is manifest by this field is part of relationship, whether we like it or not, whether it meets our needs or not. This could be children. Relatives. Friends. Associates in work and play. Indeed, it could include other intimate relationships.

The essence of relationship is not in the struggle with each other's needs but in apprehending the field that is connecting and manifesting us. There is no partnership or marriage as an assertion, only the common connection to what is generating the form of partnership or marriage. We cannot maintain the form without this field, and we cannot protect the form from what is generated next.

What we call needs are the distortions we make through our conditioning, concepts of, and resistances to this essential generative field, which is surging creatively through our system. This field we call love would suggest that we fulfill our needs without fear and guilt and fully support our partners in the fulfillment of their respective needs, with or without our participation.

Obviously, this possibility will demolish the partnership or marriage structure, which is a structure of containment, and will open up its boundaries to continuously explore fulfillment without coercion. This can release a tremendous creativity and the introduction to what is next. But what is next is change.

How does a relationship move through change without loss of the relationship itself? Again we must look to the energetic field out of which the relationship is generated and not be deluded into thinking that the relationship is generating the energetic field. The field is a changing energy, and form will mutate in the flow of this movement. Relationship will change in form, function, and expression, but if the devotion is to the energy and all that the energy manifests, then what is next is as loved as what is now.

If we suggest to ourselves and each other that we create an energy of love through our mutual admiration, our hard work on the relationship, our commitment, then we will be lost when the form changes, when the feelings change, when the relationship as we once knew it disappears into the distortion of memory.

The energy of life may remove a partner just as easily as it may bring one—or more than one—in. We will experience the expression of that energy in the movements we call our needs; in connecting to the source energy of those needs, we can discover their fulfillment. We cannot deny those energetic movements, we cannot translate them into neurotic cravings, we cannot dupe ourselves into being mindful of them, and we cannot attempt to coerce our intimates into giving expression to them on our behalf. The energy of life is knocking at our door, and we need only stop barring the door to discover what is true.

This energy is acausal, amoral, and aqualitative. It is unconcerned with what was before, with right and wrong, with like and dislike. It is raw, creative-destructive electricity.

In marriage it is the emergence of the unknown, whether it is the diagnosis of cancer or the appearance of a new partner without the loss of the first. If the partnership is anchored in the energy—if the marriage is *to* the energy—then whatever form occurs is an expression of the partnership.

This suggests that we can live completely alone and we can live intimately with multiple people. But whatever we do, it is fragmented, fearful, and reactionary if it is not sourced from the field out of which the doing itself emerges.

How do we get our needs met? What is our need, if not to be immersed in love? The variants of this essential drive—such as power, control, sex, admiration—are the conceptual or emotive interpretations of this basic need. It is ironic that these interpretations suggest a labyrinth of activities that have nothing to do with getting love, since the field of interconnectedness is always present. This field is the manifester of our needs, not the result of fulfilling them. In this respect, we can enter deeply into an engagement with even the most neurotic or apparently destructive of these elements in a post-spiritual recognition of the truth of what is actual. This contact reveals that these elements are not what they appear to the reactive interpreter, but rather what they are in actuality, an expression of the undivided whole and a bearer of transformation.

The possibility of relationship is discovered in the immersion in this energetic field and the recognition that all that flows from it is the precise manifestation of that energy. This relationship of possibility is not contained by any intention, agreement, or commitment. It lives in the edgy energy of the actual and welcomes all those who arrive for a moment or a lifetime, which as it turns out are the same.

PART 5

FORMS AND FUNCTIONS

You never change things by fighting the existing reality. To change something, build a new model that makes the existing model obsolete.
—R. Buckminster Fuller

What if we discover that our present way of life is irreconcialable with our vocation to become fully human?
—Paulo Freire

CHANGE
AS
TEMPLATE

W HAT IS NEXT IN OUR SOCIAL FORMS AND FUNCTIONS IS ENTIRELY unknown and maybe unrelated to anything we now accept as reality. How such a shift happens—whether through the advent of a new kind of human consciousness or perhaps through the collapse of the old in the large-scale trauma of war, pestilence, or ecological disaster—is speculation.

Embracing this change without resorting to utopianism, false prophets, neo- messianic leadership, political totalitarianism, or any number of forms of resistance may define the qualities with which fundamental transformation takes place.

Can we create by sourcing the actual as the foundation, change as the template, and what is next as the unlimited field of possibility? Creating, in this respect, is not science fiction or speculation, although it may read like that, but it is the engagement of our actual lives in the challenge of what is next. If this full-collision life is not compelling, then the consideration of what is possible in life will remain an entertaining fiction. If we are prepared to ride the wave of possibility rather than stand in its way, we can begin to create what is next. Creation is possibility manifest, the mystery of life made actual. Form and function are our engagement with that mystery and, even without doership, what we do is what we are.

EXPANDED FAMILIES

AND

CREATIVE PODS

I N A PURELY BIOLOGICAL WORLD, REPRODUCTIVE GROUPINGS OCCUR to ensure survival and continuation of offspring. This has no moral structure, but is instinctual in nature and reflexive in action. A troop of monkeys, a school of fish, are not in discussion of the ethics involved in their structure, they are in the action of the function.

For humans, there is the same underlying structure with the additional influence of culture. Humans group for survival and continuation, but also in response to the forces of government, religion, social mores, and family influences. This has tended to create nuclear families within varying levels of social organization, from villages to mega-cities. Polygamy, polyandry, serial monogamy, polyamory, gay partnerships, heterosexual couples, single parenting, and just plain single are all variants on the family structure, often reflecting social and economic conditions. Government and religion have been the prime forces in attempting to enforce particular forms of family and marriage structure, often punishing those who stray and thus creating underground forms imbedded in socially acceptable public forms (e.g., covert mistresses within public marriages).

The control of eros produces power for the institutions that can adequately intimidate. The byproduct is a stable societal form with all of the accompanying benefits as well as the loss of the creativity that would come with the breakdown of form. Rather than let the erotic energy loose—which would result in an unknown impact on societal structures and the truly horrifying specter, from any government's view, of a highly creative populace—eros is co-opted into commercialism. Sex sells, and we buy sex, not noticing the substitution of endless merchandise for the actual consummation with the collagen-puffed lips of the ever-attentive woman or the steroid-pumped body of the hyper-masculine man in the advertisement. To live erotically is to live as a revolutionary; sedition is punished by death. Imprisonment is left for those who don't notice that life goes by as we function without creativity.

If we are to consider post-spiritual structures, the most obvious element is that we cannot refer back to prior structures in order to continue them or to change them. We can consider the creation of structures unrelated to the past but embodying the fluid energetic movement. Rather than enforce or disassemble the family as the essential foundation of society, let us recognize its irrelevance to the question of what is next. That irrelevance does not discard the family, but recognizes it as a biological fact that is enfolded into the greater grouping around function and creation. The medieval French farmhouse included the biological family, the farmhands, and anyone else who happened to be there—a village within the village, an expression of function in form. The organizing principal was the activity of the farm, the creation of food and shelter. The biological family—while an identifiable element of the household—was not the household's identity.

The biological family has sustained itself through history and the onslaught of social engineering and economic forces. It is unlikely to go away, but just as unlikely to stay the same.

Perhaps the grouping of people around function and creativity is expressed as constructed families, not in particular biologically based families. These are families put together through mutual intention, attraction, function, or circumstance. Perhaps the basic unit of society is a creative pod, where multiple adults and children live as an extended family around the expression of co-creativity and are aligned in their energetic movement rather than in a social history. This expanded family cooperates to counter the oppressive nature of increasingly difficult economic survival. It supports the interpersonal needs of the adults, shares the challenges of parenting, and supports the young, who are entering life, and the old, who are leaving it.

This expanded family is already taking form in crude and incomplete ways. Parents share the responsibility of child rearing with daycare providers and school teachers. Adult children turn to extended care facilities and retirement homes to handle their aging parents. Adults create a series of relationships through marriage, divorce, and simple cohabitation. Often the result is a blended family with multiple second partners and their biological families all mixed in. These are all fragments of relatedness that are not melded into an integrated life. A view of relationship that includes what is new, but does not discard what is old, could bring new vitality into the expanded family. This recognizes both the conservative religious view of covenant marriage without exit and the liberal view of no-fault divorce, recognizing that both are true, but the form of historic marriage may not be.

Polygamy or polyandry among reflective and consenting adults is the fact of our culture; it is just that it is seldom done in the same time frame, in the same house, but it doesn't change the fact that most people have more than one partner in their life. We are heavily conditioned to believe that there is something wrong with multiple partners and so are obliged to discard or hide one relationship in order to enter into another. Other than superstitious belief and cultural habit, there is no obvious reason to limit family units to a man and a woman. The gay populace has made a clear case for inclusion in the form of marriage, but that is inclusion in limitation, a deal for acceptance where the price is state and religious license and control of human relatedness. Like the inclusion of women in the military, it is a pyrrhic victory to be accepted into the ranks of destruction.

Why are the state and the church involved with the regulation of human relatedness? Many of our social structures are designed to control the sensual/sexual/erotic expression, and we have sublimated these controls into our psyche of separation, jealousy, and insecurity. If creativity is to flow in these new social forms, then eros may also flow. More than one attempt at these social experiments has failed due to the confusion that arises when sexuality meets the utopian ideal. Without the ideals and without the social restrictions, what is the actuality of this energy as it applies not to the restriction of a couple, but to an extended group? Does it naturally seek expression in a monogamous pair? Does it structure in a particular way around male and female? What are the actual parameters of the creative expression in relationship when we are not limited to the historic views of religion or government?

We cannot assume, simply because these restrictions have been in place, that they are a complete description of the human potential, nor can we assume that we have the natural capacity to step beyond the teachings and mores of these historic institutions. We can inquire together as to the possibility of social mutation; we can approach the edges of our capacities and the possibility of expanded relationship in service of life itself. The milieu of discovery will be relationships anchored in the actual, where the very basis of a life together is the recognition that it is a life of discovery and openness.

Could society build around culturally creative pods, each interlinked with the other? Can our world organize in an interrelated communion rather than a hierarchical power structure? Will each of us place our life in that question and risk it all to find out?

We now live in relative isolation, perhaps making do with a partner, a few offspring, and a tenuous hold on the idea of security in holding a job and getting by. We could open the door of our life to the flow of the world, invite in others with whom we can create, and begin to work not for security but for creativity and joy. Our past tells us this is not possible, and the past is often right in its predictions. But we will only know if we discover what is possible, take the risk of creativity, and find in failure the invitation to go deeper.

LEARNING
COMMUNITIES

T HE CHILD IS DESIGNED TO TAKE IN THE UNIVERSE, CONSUME IT, AND transform it into growth and intelligence. Education, as we know it, is so enamored with producing results that it is neither teaching nor learning; it is containment of that unfettered energy of childhood.

Rather than focus on stuffing more information into our children's overloaded brains, what if we bring the attention of children into the space in which they actually exist, the fact of relatedness? We cannot force children into the awareness of that inter-relatedness; we can demonstrate it in our lives, and that should keep us busy enough that we won't damage children with our coercive and violent ideas of education.

Learning communities might be built around the creative pods to support the self-directed learning of the young and as a continuous invitation to those of all ages to learn and to teach as an integral part of the day-to-day life. Traditional schools have failed for so long and are so obviously better placed in the nineteenth century, where they came from, that we can look to what is next without considering schools as being in the least relevant.

As a prime function of the human potential, learning—like creativity—can spawn structures that support and express that potential. Learning has nothing in particular to do with school buildings, compulsory education, certified teachers, or the multi-billion-dollar government-industrial cartel that supports these structures at the expense of those who pay and those who suffer the fiasco we call education. Actual learning needs only the material resources of a basic life, access to the flow of information, and mentors that make up a society formed to learn, to teach, and to support the natural unfolding of the human potential.

Education has come to mean a kind of mass panic, a psychosis of fear that our children are not keeping up, that they will fail as adults unless we constantly threaten them with failure as children. We try so hard to make children achieve without fully explaining to them or ourselves what it is that they are to achieve and why. Success is the ability to have more than most, to afford health care, to own a house, to own a nice car. Yet when you add all of that up, for most it doesn't make a life; it makes a car payment, a mortgage payment, a health insurance payment, and credit card payments in the endless pursuit of security.

It is difficult to even introduce the notion that learning is not best served by solely and slavishly attending to intellectual development. We are infatuated with the idea that overdeveloping the intellectual is directly related to a good life. Perhaps this was true in the past, but it is not the case when we look at the actual challenge in the life that is next.

The deficiencies of the intellect can only be remedied by the complete development of human intelligence, a quality that can be defined only by admitting that we know only a little about what that might be. We have indications that some human capacities are not being served well by contemporary education, and these we can list (emotional, social, artistic, creative, intuitive, and so forth), but that list will never fully describe what is missing. We can say in simplest terms that we do not teach or learn to live in flow—the optimum state of learning and creativity. We see examples of those who live and work in this quality of full attention and concentration along with heightened space awareness and temporal plasticity, like the professional athlete, the charismatic actor, the performing musician. We see this quality in young children at play, yet we educate to remove this capacity, to reign in the exuberance of the young, and mold them into a more standardized component of society. There is mounting evidence that a large portion of young learning takes place in play and in sleep, areas our society is fond of restricting.

A learning community that lives in its flow, made of components built around function and creativity, could be structured to support the young and old in their continued exploration of a full life. If life is as it appears—acausal—then life itself is at play. Learning, as play, is both the expression of this fundamental actuality and the exploration of life's deepest mysteries. Spirituality seldom deals with play, although Jesus did suggest the attributes of children as necessary to enter the Kingdom of God. Historically the masters' advice to various acolytes gave a view of the spiritual process as a grim undertaking, demanding austerities and withdrawal, certainly not a family life.

The learning community is charged with the manifestation of the human potential. This is not a life centered on a passive relationship to culture and the acquisition of things in substitution for the missing relatedness. Rather, the learning community cultivates a collective of cultural creatives from cradle to grave as the essence of its social meaning.

The historic society that is now cracking apart can only understand in fragments: home, workplace, school, government, and so forth. It can combine fragments into larger fragments like a city, a state, and a country. The conditioning of fragmentation, the education of compartmentalization, the biology of competition does not allow for a holistic view or for the creation of an integral culture. That is not the challenge, in any event. Let us not be distracted by the notion of reforming what doesn't work, rather let us engage in what begets an integral life: the biology of transcendence, the culture of creativity, and integral learning guided by curiosity and relatedness.

THE BUSINESS
OF LIVING

A CULTURE OF CREATIVITY IMPACTS THE CURRENT OUTMODED SOCI-
etal structure not by confronting it, but by ignoring it. It is
the perception of irrelevance that is the most powerful force of
change. The age of revolution is over, and that of sudden and
unpredictable paradigm shift is upon us. All institutions—gov-
ernmental, religious, and business—are held together and
empowered by belief and energized by resistance. The new
revolutionaries are those who step into the creative flow to
generate the future culture now by simply living it.
Commercialism fails when no one buys; wars end when no
one is willing to fight; dictators fall when citizens cease coop-
erating. When belief shifts, change occurs. When belief
becomes fluid, change is a constant possibility and culture
becomes creative.

The rise of fundamentalism is the resistance to the breakdown in belief, but once broken through, belief becomes only
a subset of a higher order, one that fundamentalism cannot
understand. From this new perspective, fundamentalism is
seen as a force that creates its own opposite and thrives on
conflict. Christian fundamentalists will forget their Christ's
instructions of love to attack Islamic fundamentalists, who will
fight back, forgetting that their prophet came to extend the
Judeo-Christian religion to the pagan tribes of Arabia. Ethnic

group fights ethnic group. Left fights right. Country fights country.

Or not. *Not* is the shift, and *not* is the possibility and opening to what is next. What may become clear is that wars are never won, conflicts never finished. Belief in this is like belief in that—still stuck in a fragmented view that resists dialog and communion. As the perception of *global* penetrates the belief systems of separation, what opens up is not a new belief, but the ending of belief as a guide.

Corporations are the dinosaurs of our world culture, great plodding beasts, powerful, unstoppable—and doomed because they cannot adapt. They depend on an intricate mass hypnosis that has created a feudal system so convincing in its illusion that the serfs gladly work for the warlords with hardly a murmur about the inequities that seem so obvious. Yet with all their apparent power, the corporations are fragile constructions. The lives of the largest of them are typically measured in mere decades before they collapse, are sold, taken over, or parted out. The structures themselves are not sustainable, nor are their products, nor the culture that grows from them. The corporations are missing the agility to change or, for that matter, to even perceive change. They are born and they grow in aggressive creativity and die on the momentum of structures so inflexible and brittle as to be unresponsive to the rapidly mutating marketplace. These organizations' inability to change is the very element that will create change.

We have given the corporation bizarre features: we consider the corporation to have the legal status of a person; those within a corporation are free of liability for the corporate actions; the top of the large corporation is paid in the millions to reduce the bottom wages to the minimum possible. The list of strange attributes of the corporation is rather long, and yet this odd form is considered normal, indeed desirable.

The corporation could serve the deepest aspirations of those who work in it, those who capitalize it, those who buy from it, and the whole of the community at large. That, of course, would require change, and corporations can't change, just as individuals can't change, as we have seen. These are created realities, stuck in their form, mechanical in their movements, with no escape. Change will come, not be created, and what cannot move with it will fall away.

The corporation could transform itself by disregarding its own reality and its own limitations. Why doesn't a corporation function as a creative pod, a learning community of those who co-create every day? Why doesn't a corporation embody the ambition to be sustainable, humane, charitable, and profitable, as an organization, for each of its members and in its contribution to the community at large? The corporate structure doesn't stand in the way, nor does the individual who works or owns the corporation. Only the belief in the reality of this intertwined structure limits the potential transformation. That belief only stands in the way now. What is next is open to all possibilities.

The movement of life is not embodied in one culture over another, one political system over another. While our evangelical fervor for democracy sends us on crusades to bring the vote to the masses of the world, it is not clear why the universe would have a particular interest in democracy. Voting is a fine and efficient way to relieve social tensions, but in the end it takes the unique voice of many and subsumes it into a one-size-fits-all conclusion. Anyone experienced with young children knows that confronting their will is a disaster, but giving the child a choice will both divert their attention and give them the illusion that they are in control. *You must eat your vegetables* is likely to create an uprising in the streets, but *Do you want to eat peas or do you want to eat carrots?* will bring the young revolutionary into the political process and sublimate the reaction into acceptable behavior.

Democracy is a pragmatic form but hardly the final chapter in discovering the social expression of the human potential. Democracy is an ideal; the actual is something else entirely. Like all forms of social governance, democracy is subject to the stresses of what underlies it. It too must change, but cannot.

Can a society be run without creating winners and losers, without an either/or mentality—a system where the majority rules and the minority is ruled? If democracy results in dominance, do the means justify the end? We say that it is an imperfect system but the best that we have. But the imperfections of democracy are imbedded in the system itself, and the system is a reality, unable to change, like all realities. Yet change is creating what is next, and those who live in that energy may find little that is relevant in the democracies of today. The irony of artificial democracies is that the most powerful vote is the one that is not cast. What if they had a democracy and no one came? Consensus, theocracy, anarchy, libertarianism are all theories of what is possible now, but none take into account the mutation of the individual and the potential of co-creation of what is next.

The human biological structure is itself a thought system encoded in and communicating from the complexities of the molecular level. Our bodies and minds are not two, but one, flowing through not just the synaptic structures of the brain, but neural tissue elsewhere in the body and the peptide network in organs, skin, muscle, and endocrine glands—embodying thought and emotion in a dynamic structure that is change personified. These structures are not fixed, but subject to mutation. Living structures have the ability to correct flawed genetic material; in short, we have the capacity to change, and to change instantly and radically.

Thought is static, the thought of *me* is entirely fixed, but what we are in actuality is dynamic, an expression of an energetic universe and an unlimited potential.

CO-CREATION

WE ABANDONED THE SELF TO ENTER INTO A UNITARY CONDITION, and now we are left abandoned by the unitary state, abandoned by all states—the price we pay to give expression to the co-creation of life. It costs us our sense of self, of meaning, of time, of security, and leaves us in an aqualitative world where our likes and dislikes are irrelevant. We have no morality to guide us. We recognize nothing predictable or mechanical in the quantum reality we now inhabit. Fear does not inhibit us, rather we utilize this as energy to manifest in the face of nonexistence. We are the creating force, but not creators; rather we are Creators, capitalized and plural to indicate both source and the multiplicity of form, a singularity and plurality.

Co-creation is what is left when all else falls away, and what is next is its creation. The human potential lies in this realm and beyond. It is largely untapped, as we live out of a small sliver of our true range of capacity.

Every aspect of what we know and what we hold onto as our life may undergo vast shift. The beginning point is in the shift of our conceptual world, a structure we have believed to be a concrete representation of the world, but which we may now see as an imaginary projection of a virtual world. Our ideas are fixed and, in that structure, a world of possibility is impossible. Yet, the impossible is emerging in ever surprising ways, confusing our surety and simultaneously introducing both the actual of manifestation and the quantum potential of what is next.

Wherever we are and whatever our circumstance, we are each an agent of and an ineffable expression of the co-creative energetic flow, the mutation of the present into what is next after now.

ABOUT THE AUTHOR

Steven Harrison is the author of *Doing Nothing, The Question to Life's Answers, Being One, Getting to Where You Are,* and *The Happy Child.*

Those interested may write:

Steven Harrison
P O Box 6071
Boulder, CO 80306
InDialog@aol.com
www.doingnothing.com

Sentient Publications, LLC publishes books on cultural creativity, experimental education, transformative spirituality, holistic health, new science, ecology, and other topics, approached from an integral viewpoint. Our authors are intensely interested in exploring the nature of life from fresh perspectives, addressing life's great questions, and fostering the full expression of the human potential. Sentient Publications' books arise from the spirit of inquiry and the richness of the inherent dialogue between writer and reader.

We are very interested in hearing from our readers. To direct suggestions or comments to us, or to be added to our mailing list, please contact:

SENTIENT PUBLICATIONS, LLC
1113 Spruce Street
Boulder, CO 80302
303-443-2188
contact@sentientpublications.com
www.sentientpublications.com